PRAISE FOR '
WITH GOD A
BY DEBRA LEE FADER

MW01289610

"Debra Lee Fader's *Walk by Faith with God as Your Compass* is a good read. I love her book. Debra Lee is a former Mayor, International Singing Star, and Broadcaster. There are quotes from the Bible that say, "You will know them by their love, fruits, joy, and deeds." This is the essence, as Debra Lee conveys compassion and connection to people. Also, the impact of positive leadership and community, with respect for all spiritual principles. Debra Lee was stricken with a debilitating illness and has put *Mind over Matter* to succeed. The message is great and beautiful." *-Jack Canfield* #1 New York Times Bestselling Author of *Chicken Soup for the Soul Series* and *The Success Principles*

"Debra Lee is an AMAZING person. When you talk to Debra, she is always full of wisdom. She has poured all her wisdom into this book. I recommend everyone to read it. Get inspired to *Walk by Faith*. -**Nathalie Nkashama**, Global Impact Center-USA

"Debra Lee has a fighting spirit and a supernatural faith that moves mountains. Do not miss her compelling story!" *-Rachel Mastrogiacomo,* Mastro's on Mission

"I love Debra Lee and her positive outlook on life. Her "Walk by Faith" book reflects her all-encompassing walk with Jesus. Read her book and be inspired to "Walk by Faith" as well." **-Rev Dr. Paul Marzhan** CROSSROADS Multi-Site Church

"Debra Lee's life experiences have been so amazing. Working with Debra on musical and dramatic productions is rewarding for everyone within all community diversities. Everything she has learned, and shares will be invaluable to all readers." **-Ruth Ann Lee**, Proprietor-Hollywood on Main LLC

"Debra's life is an amazing story of faith, love, courage, and overcoming impossible obstacles. Her story will inspire you to trust God, seize hope, and do the impossible in your life." **-Dr. Larry Keefauver**, Bestselling Author and International Teacher

WALK BY

FAITH

WALK BY

FAITH

WITH GOD AS YOUR COMPASS

DEBRA LEE FADER

XULON ELITE

Xulon Press Elite
555 Winderley Pl, Suite 225
Maitland, FL 32751
407.339.4217
www.xulonpress.com

Unless otherwise indicated, Scripture quotations taken from the King James Version (KJV)—public domain.

Paperback ISBN-13: 978-1-66284-682-3
Hard Cover ISBN-13: 978-1-66289-511-1
Dust Jacket ISBN-13: 978-1-66289-512-8
Ebook ISBN-13: 978-1-66284-683-0

DEDICATION

This book is dedicated to the memories of my mother, Marlene Ell-Jorgensen, and my father, Robert W. Jorgensen. Also, to my beloved husband, Bradley Fader. Not to forget my precious family, and irreplaceable friends.

*For the carousel, to reaching for the big brass ring, going beyond, and taking hold of **God as Your Compass**.*

Acknowledgements

HOW DO YOU *begin to thank each person who has given something toward your life? You just have to try…It is truly impossible…Only God knows. At this point, I refer to the first sentence of the Nicene Creed:*

"We believe in one God, the Father, the Almighty, Maker
of heaven and earth, of all that is Seen and Unseen."

Frankly, our lives are full of moments where we can clearly see the workings of God. However, what about the moments we cannot see? The people who are part of the fabric of your life, that you never knew were shaping your journey. Let me start with my appreciation for the unseen people and unseen contributions that have helped me through this journey called life. My humblest thank you for your generosity and effort, on my behalf.

Some of the people listed within this missive of acknowledgements may no longer be alive. Since I am still alive, they will be listed, as it is the honorable thing to do.

There are so many wonderful people who have shaped me with unconditional love. Of course, my parents, Bob and Marlene Jorgensen. So much gratitude for my brother Rick Jorgensen. For Rick's sons, Blake Jorgensen, Travis Jorgensen, and their families. For my sister, Shelley O Hansen and her husband Kyle Hansen. For Rachel and Richie Mastrogiacomo, and family, Also, Tori and Jason Harless, and family. For Billy Olson and his bride, Maddie.

Grateful credit to Michael Olson for helping to shape a more concise message within one of my chapters. Thank you for acknowledging our positive energy, VJ Fehoko. For Jacob Olson and his Bride, Sheridan. Also, I am blessed by the memory of Bill Olson.

In memory of my Godparents, Bob and Marjorie Christian. In 2022, we lost our Patriarch, Bob Jorgensen. We also lost cousin Mike Christian. For memories of Uncle Gary Brown. Also, cousin John Brown, who died in 2023. While our family grieves loss, I wish to express love for Deborah Wentz Allison. For Mike's daughter, Amanda. For Mike's son Mic, Kali and family. Love to cousins Greg and Sherrie Christian, Daniel, Jeremiah and Duke. For Matt and Sarah Pikus and family.

During 2024, we lost our Matriarch, Marlene Ell Jorgensen. Again, as we grieve loss, our hearts reach out with love for our Ell family and cousins, Roberta Harvey, and Shannon Ortega.

In memory of Kathy Jorgensen. Gratefulness for Bob Wilson. Also, Tim and Denise Wilson, Devin and Ian.

*Thanks to Joaquin Alvarez from USIU, for encouraging me to stay in school and finish my degree. Thanks to the **Broadway Toppers**. A shout out to my co-worker, Randy Brown. Randy and I shared the stage together as members of **BDT Toppers**, **Lido de Paris** and **Miller Reich Productions**.*

*Without Adelaide Robbins, my audition for **Lido de Paris**, would not have sparkled. Profound appreciation for **Lido de Paris** production creators-Donn Arden, and Madame Bluebell (Margaret Kelly). I also shine a positive light upon the risk-taking and calculating persistence of Mr. Frank Rosenthal. In 1978, Mr. Rosenthal contracted **Siegfried and Roy** to Headline at the Stardust in **Lido de Paris**. Collaborating in this new agreement was **SR** Personal Manager, Bernie Yuman. With the stroke of a pen, a new era in Las Vegas Entertainment began. This pioneering move ensured that **Siegfried and Roy-Superstars of Magic**, would catapult into an ever-growing Iconic Brand personifying Las Vegas, prior to, and during the new millennium. I am so grateful to have witnessed **SR's** initial rise to stardom, and to have shared the stage in **Lido de Paris**.*

Complete appreciation for **Miller Reich Productions**. *For the memories of George Reich and Leonard Miller. Thank you to Pat Merl, Sharon Michalko, Glenda Grainger, Brenda Bonterre, Cal Warren, Hamid Azize, Moises Gomes, Anita Fuentes, and Michael Barone. For the memory of Luis Vigoreaux, and his broadcasted variety show on WAPA 4, San Juan, Puerto Rico. For the memory of Leon Altemose, previous proprietor of Sheraton Valley Forge Hotel. Special love to cast members from Puerto Rico and Valley Forge, PA. We were a family. Grateful for Robin Sheridan, Susan Nesbit-Blanco, Dana Warner-Logan, Vicki Smith, Judi Millet, Gayle Mcdonald, Khali Loinaz-Azize, Debra Nelson, Debbie "Zip" Zimmerman-VanMeter, Olga Matarrese, Maryjane Schram, Debra Gayle, Kristine Keppel, Cookie Ramos, Kelly King, Todd Rinehart, and so many others.*

Eventually, I had dreams of having my own act. Many Specialty Acts encouraged me. Thank you to Goldfinger and Dove, Anibal De Leon, Los Huincas Gauchos, and Halls of Magic. In memory of Senor Wences, The Great Tomsoni & Company, and Ken Noyle.

Thank you, Irv Gordon, for your orchestral arrangements. Most appreciative of Yurij Pencak for your musical collaboration on land and sea, throughout the '80's. Humble thankfulness to Paul Lowden, Bernie Yuman, Ron Andrews, and Jon Boni from Sahara and Hacienda Hotels, Las Vegas. in memory of Tommy Hodges, and Henry Lackey from Sahara and Hacienda Hotels, Las Vegas. Much appreciation for Morris Shenker and family, and the Dunes Hotel. Many thanks to the Radisson Hotel Chain and Holiday Inn Hotels. Thank you for Taylor Reed and Bobby Reed. Both of you helped so much in promoting my techno-dance record.

Gracious thanks to Atlantic City - Trump Castle, Trump Plaza, Resorts International, Harrah's, and Tropicana Resorts. Thank you, MGM, Reno. Thank you, Harrah's Laughlin. In memory of Ruby La Placa, manager for Windows on Hollywood. Thank you, NCL-Cunard, RCL-Disney Cruise Lines, and Carnival Cruise Lines. Much love to my many Cruise Lines Shipmates, from all over the world! Cheers to the many exceptional, talented, and resourceful human beings I worked with while at sea. My gratefulness to the core unit of Shipmates organizing "Reunions at Sea", in order to keep our friendships alive. They are Trudi Kaye, Osvaldo and Cheryl De Paula, and Juanita Martindale. Thank you for flying "across the pond", three times to visit me, Ali Cantelo!

Settling again in my home state of Minnesota has brought more abundance than I ever could have imagined. God has thoroughly blessed me with more family, more friends and more valuable mentors. Being presented with so much goodness, opportunity, and guidance, is truly a "God Thing."

Living in Montevideo brought me my husband Brad Fader, his family and close friends. Having two more sisters and a brother is a delight. In appreciation for Tammy Fader Ryan and her daughters. For Jayme and Mark Wrolstad and family. For Brooke and Nick Marsh, and family. Gratefulness to Dori Fader Jackson, son Anthony Jackson and family. Also, to Tarey Fader and family.

Having more cousins is also a blessing. Gratefulness for Cindy and Jeff Burgess, their children, Cassie, Seth, and Isaac. Both Cassie and Seth have families of their own. More family ties with Greg Rude, Connie DeVries, and daughters, Heidi and Brianne, including their families. Also, Jan and Debbie DeVries, including family. Not to forget Roma Kindshi, the Mortenson family, and additional members of the Fader family, such as Bob and Carol Fader, and more. Also, the Blake family. Now is the time to acknowledge the "Fader's Raiders", (you know who you are). Thank you for so graciously accepting me into your loyal circle of fun and friendship. A huge shout out to the Grandparents Tribe: G-G-ma Mary, Brad, Bev, Ron, Kathy, Randy and AJ. Missing KT, hoping to see Cassie and Waylon.

Ever grateful for broadcasting colleagues Tim Burns, Deanna Hodge, Roger Hill, Dwight Mulder, Roberta Kuno, Paul Raymo, Maynard Meyer, Terry Overlander, Lou Kuno and others. For the memory of Andy Coulter.

For a while, I worked as a department manager at the Montevideo Walmart Supercenter. We truly worked as a team. All co-workers were a tight knit family. Many are now retired, but I have to say that I still cannot leave that store without seeing old friends.

Will never forget Derrick Schiff, Barb Morseth, Mr. and Mrs. Keith Hein, the Pauline family, various prayer groups, and the Montevideo Ministerium. Much obliged to Montevideo, MN citizens, former City Manager Steve Jones, Montevideo City Hall Staff, Montevideo Police Department, Montevideo Fire Department, Montevideo City Council, EDA, MIDC, and Montevideo Area Chamber of Commerce.

In appreciation for Montevideo American News, Mike Dupree, Jeremy Jones, Jessica Stolen-Jacobson, Samantha Godfrey and so many others. Grateful to Tom Cherveny at West Central Tribune. Complete appreciation for Chicago Consulate of Uruguay, now serving as Uruguayan Ambassador to Malaysia, Dr. Elsa Nury Bauzan-Benzano. Gracias to former Mayor Ana Olivera representing Montevideo, Uruguay. Many thanks to Montevideo Convention and Visitors Bureau, Fiesta Days Board, Federico Estol, Patrick Moore, Eric Brand, Robert Scarlett, US State Department, and Uruguayan Partners of the Americas.

*Complete appreciation for past and present Diversity-USA Advisory Board. Especially, Sandy Lynn Erickson, Karen Stegeman, Nancy Feldhake, Jammie Niemeyer, Leo Baker, Wyatt Haugen, Adrian Walstrom, Pastor Linda Estling and Nathalie Nkashama. **A very special thank you to my sister from another mother, Ruth Ann Lee.** Ruth Ann, Jerry and their family have brought so much joy to Central Minnesota by holding events at **Hollywood on Main, LLC**. Applause for the emcees, musicians, speakers, dancers, singers, volunteers, and tech crews. Thank you, Mediapolis, and Special Touch Videography. Also, Mark Bohler Photography.*

*The impetus to write this book started at the **Lido de Paris-All Cast Reunion** in Paris, France.*

Sentimental thanks go out to Show Biz Friends coordinator, Lindsey Raven, her husband Sergio Rosolino, and their son, Christian Rosolino. Reminiscing with so many former cast members and performers from all over the world was outstanding. This life changing event gave me courage to put down in words the moments in my life, making me who I am today. Merci beaucoup-Athena

Patacsil, and Sheri Lewis, for interviewing me, on your respective Podcasts. Due to these Podcasts, I started my own. **Recipe for Kindness**. Many thanks to Jeremiah Christian, for past Celebrity Chef Segments. Also, my deep appreciation for Jordan Gulbranson and Cory Soine, as you both have shared your technical skills and live collaboration.

Trying to write in the middle of the Covid-19 World Pandemic was akin to drawing blood out of a turnip. During this time, my goals shifted to Chaplain Certification and Ordination. Grateful thanks to Dr. Alfred Phillips from Anointed By God Ministries and International Fellowship of Chaplains.

For years, I had been corresponding with Steve and Bill Harrison, about writing a book. My writing project would never have gotten off the ground without the guidance of Bradley Communications. With special thanks to Joe McCallister, Claire Doney, Raia King, Laura Harrison, Danette Kubanda, Debra Englander, Christina Smith, Geoffrey Berwind, Brian Edmondson, Nick Summa, Carl Bussler, Dr. Lee Johnson, Dan Holland, Kimberley Cruse, Cynthia Janzen and technical support staff.

Steve Harrison facilitated the introduction to Jack Canfield. In 2022-23, I committed to write a chapter for **The Keys to Authenticity-Unlocking the Code** with Jack Canfield. In 2023-24, I followed up with writing a chapter in **Rise Up!** with Lisa Nichols. Both books are Certified Best Sellers! My sincere appreciation to Nick Nanton, JW Dicks, Zack Viscomi, Jason (JT) Thomas, Guy Colangelo, Mandy Tawbush, Angie Swenson, Matt Whitman, Ryan Ruff, Michaela Virto and all Staff at Celebrity Press and Success Books.

Thank you to the founder of Sponsorship Concierge, Linda Hollander. Prayerful acknowledgement for Entrepreneur Soul Coach, Sasha Sabbeth. Great appreciation for Cash CEO Business Tips from Belinda and Marc Rosenblum. Gratitude for networking with Jason Kanigan at Cold Star Technologies

For website development and internet tech assistance, my gratitude to Debbie Girvan, Nina Palmares, Angelica Billones, RJ Villanueva, Anthony Anderson, Shane Dowdy, and Maia Taketa. Complete thanks to my Administrative Assistant, Nepthaly F. Anthony.

Lastly, Steve Harrison also paved the way to meet Nat Mundel, CEO of Voyage Media and Films. Thank you, Voyage Media and Staff for combining efforts to write an adaptive screenplay, from the stories told in **Walk By Faith with God as Your Compass***.*

My most sincere ambition entailed finishing this book. It has taken nearly three and a half years to complete!! Soulful gratitude to Xulon Press, for the faith-based validation I needed, in order to keep on writing. Xulon Press has been with me every step of the way. Many thanks to Lisa Waters, Logan Mungo, Dr. Larry Keefauver, Jesse Kline, Michelle Ramos, Erica Coulter, and Regan Sanders. Additionally, my thanks to the unknown workers at Xulon Press, pouring over this project during production. A big thank you to Amanda Weisel at Palmer Creations in Glenwood, MN.

FYI: No doubt, it would have been impossible to complete this task without the support and noble vision of my editor, Dr. Larry Keefauver. Thank you for taking me under your wing - guiding me to remain steadfast.

A heartfelt thank you to our son Jason Fader Christopherson, wife Mandy, children Jules and Miles, for all your love, support, and memories during this project. Each of you are so loved.

Finally, my eternal humility and deepest appreciation is for you, dear Reader. My infinite gratitude to you for offering up a bit of your precious time to read or listen to my story. May You Always Be Blessed by Almighty God.

TABLE OF CONTENTS

INTRODUCTION

I'VE FALLEN AND CAN'T GET UP...REALLY!

RIGHT BEFORE CHRISTMAS *in 2006, the fall came! I had been having some problems earlier in the summer with my left foot. The foot kept falling asleep, but I would just shake it off. Then, go swimming, go to work and to continue to live my life. I really didn't give it much thought.*

Shortly before Christmas, I went to get out of bed and I fell to my knees, and then I fell on my face. I couldn't move anything. My hands were almost at the sides of my face. I was just face planted on the ground. From the elbows and forearms down, I was able to move my wrists and hands. I was lucky to be able to pull myself with my fingernails and hands, using as much of my arm area straining to get to a nearby phone. I was laying on my belly trying to move forward. The rest of my body and arms had no feeling. I finally got to the phone.

First, I called my husband, Brad and I said, "I can't move. Something is desperately wrong."

He said, "I'll be there as soon as I can be. You better call work so they're not waiting for you."

I called work and I told my manager, "I can't walk. I am laying on the floor."

He said, "Oh, you are? Well then, just crawl in here and tell me all about it."

I said, "No, I'm serious. I can't move."

I was taken to the emergency room, but they couldn't do anything for me. They didn't know what to do.

For almost ten years, nobody knew what was wrong with me. Misdiagnosed, misunderstood, and mistaken for a fake, I felt all alone, but for God…and He was most silent and not healing me despite my prayer and faith.

What had just happened to me?
What was I to do or not to do?
Who could help me?
Who knows what to do for me?
Why had this happened to me?

My journey to rising after falling revealed many life lessons about myself, my family and friends, my work colleagues, my doctors and therapists, and most of all about God. Take the journey with me and learn lifesaving tips for not just surviving but for thriving….

Body and Soul
I Am Wonderfully Made

God, investigate my life; get all the facts firsthand.
I'm an open book to you; even from a distance, you know what I'm thinking.
You know when I leave and when I get back;
I'm never out of your sight.
You know everything I'm going to say before I start the first sentence.
I look behind me and you're there, then up ahead and you're there, too
— your reassuring presence, coming and going.
This is too much, too wonderful — I can't take it all in!
Is there anyplace I can go to avoid your Spirit? to be out of your sight?
If I climb to the sky, you're there!
If I go underground, you're there!
If I flew on morning's wings to the far western horizon,
You'd find me in a minute — you're already there waiting.
Then I said to myself, "Oh, he even sees me in the dark!
At night I'm immersed in the light!"
It's a fact: darkness isn't dark to you; night and day, darkness and light,
they're all the same to you.
Oh yes, you shaped me first inside, then out;
you formed me in my mother's womb.
I thank you, High God — you're breathtaking!
Body and soul, I am marvelously made!
I worship in adoration — what a creation!
You know me inside and out,
you know every bone in my body;
You know exactly how I was made, bit by bit,
how I was sculpted from nothing into something.
Like an open book, you watched me grow from conception to birth;
all the stages of my life were spread out before you,
The days of my life all prepared before I'd even lived one day.
(Psalm 139:1-17 MSG)

CHAPTER 1 PART 1

GOD HAS GOOD PLANS FOR YOUR FUTURE

LOOK AT THE poetic psalm I quoted to the left of this page. From as early I can remember I believed I was special to God and to my parents. He had created me to be his masterpiece. After much labor, Friday the Thirteenth's "Luckiest Child" was born in Seattle, Washington in 1954, in King County at the Military Hospital. My parents had recently returned from a Tour of Duty in Japan. When I was nine days old, we flew back to Minnesota and settled in Bloomington. I was a happy little girl with bundles of love and musical talent.

My favorite part of every morning was to wake up, to turn on our black and white TV. I would sit on the sofa and wait for the station sign on. Then, Mahalia Jackson would sing hymns. Mahalia Jackson and her singing was always a part of the first hour of programming, as I recall. My heart was set on becoming Mahalia Jackson when I grew up. This dream was an indelible part of my soul. She had a very big voice, and she sang my favorite hymns. Nothing could remove my dream of being Mahalia.

Then, at night, I could watch Dinah Shore. I knew the TV Jingle for the Chevrolet Car by heart! It started like this, "See the USA in your Chevrolet" …the tag ending was, "so make a date today to see the USA and see it in your Chevrolet." I knew I had to grow up to be Dinah Shore, too!

1

I learned very early by age three, that I could sing either like a "big lady singer" or a "little girl singer." I would sing all over the house "big lady" style. Then, with my friends, in church or with classmates, I would sing "little girl" style. Didn't want to rock the boat with my peers.

At three I began dance classes. Dance was my greatest love of all-especially tap dancing. All about the rhythm. Using my feet and legs as though they were playing the drums. Nothing but music for me!

Another milestone in my life was at three and a half years old. In order to keep me occupied during the winter so that she could do her housework, my mother would allow me to watch the Matinee Movie in the afternoon on television. On one snowy day, I watched a movie named "Grand Hotel." Greta Garbo was in the movie. She played the role of a Prima Ballerina, and I was entranced with her.

When my father came home from work that evening, I ran to him and gave him a big hug. Then, I ran into my bedroom and shut the door. My dad settled in and called for me to come back out. I did not reappear. Growing worried, he knocked on my door. I refused to answer. Then, he opened the door, to find out if I was okay.

I looked up at him and said, "I VANT to be ALONE!"

Dad remarked, "YOU are SO DRAMATIC!"

As he chuckled to himself, he called out to my mother, "Honey, we have a little actress on our hands."

Then, he quietly closed the door so that I could be alone until dinnertime. Thus, I knew my calling. I was going to grow up to be Mahalia, Dinah, and Greta Garbo…

We were a praying family. I said my prayers every night and at meals. We went to church on Sunday. I had a huge faith in God as a youngster.

God put my faith in my dreams,
and nothing could shake my faith in God.
God had good plans for my future!
God would give me the ability to accomplish my dreams.

Our family grew. My age was three and a half, while waiting with undying love for my first baby brother to be born. Bobby was here on this earth for one week. The power of Jesus and heaven was all around me, while experiencing the pain of Bobby's sudden death. A year later, Rick was born! My heart became full again! Then, Shelley was born! What unbridled joy! Having both a brother and a sister was truly, my miracle. The summer flew by, and I was finally six years old. Time to start school.

I went to Parochial School first through third grade. We had classes in Quonset hut trailers because an addition was being constructed onto our church for grade schoolers. There were no windows in the hut trailers.

We had family friends whose son would always have nosebleeds in school. My job was to take care of his nosebleeds whenever he had one. So, my teacher had me sitting in the back of the room, next to him. Prepared to take care of him whenever he had a nosebleed. We were way in the back of the classroom, very near a small break room. If my classmate had a nosebleed, I'd have to take care of him, and bring him into the breakroom, so he could lay down. Then, clean up the mess. The teacher would come to the breakroom and check on us, but just kept on teaching the class.

Since our tables and chairs were so far back in the classroom, I couldn't see the writing on the blackboard. I couldn't see the letters of the alphabet above the blackboard. Everything was always a blur for me at school. My teachers and the nuns told my parents that I was at best, a grade C student and would be so all my years in school.

I complained to my parents that I didn't think I could see everything in the classroom, but the nuns convinced my parents that I could see. Both of my parents had excellent vision. Why would my vision be less than perfect? There was no need to doubt the teachers. The nuns would expound upon me with discipline, for my lack of understanding of the school subjects. I would listen hard and that is how I learned.

My parents put me in Public School for the fourth grade. No more carpools to the Catholic School. I could walk the block to my new school. Since seats were not automatically assigned, I found that if I arrived at school early enough, I could sit in the front row. While sitting in the front row, I could see the letters on the blackboard. My schoolwork improved. I was overall so much happier! Miss Lewis was my fourth-grade teacher. She recognized my musical abilities and placed me in the Bloomington All-City Student Choir. She also placed me in the Bloomington All-City Student Council. Miss Lewis told my parents I was more than a grade C student. She also said my greatest strength was the willingness to cooperate.

I walked to school every morning with Laurie. We lived on the same street and played together all of the time. Then, all of a sudden, Laurie stopped going to school. A month passed by, and Miss Lewis would give me homework to bring to Laurie's house. Laurie never came to the door, but the homework was always finished when I would take it back to school.

Soon, Laurie came back to class. Her parents brought her to school, twice in a week. At the end of the day, we walked home together. Our talks were very serious as we walked. She would ask me if I believed in God. My answer was, "Yes, Laurie, I believe in God." "How can you be sure?", she'd ask. I would say that I just believed. Then we would stop along the way home to watch the birds. We'd pick up the leaves falling from the trees. Another question she asked me about was heaven. "Do you believe we go to heaven when we die?", she'd ask. "Yes, Laurie, I believe that we go to heaven", I'd say. "How do you know?", she'd ask. My answer to her was, "Because my heart tells me so." Laurie would say nothing else. Sometimes, she'd run ahead of me. I'd catch up. We'd continue to walk in silence.

Over a year later, after playing outside in the summer, after shuttling many sheets of homework paper, and after having a great sleepover with many girls at Laurie's house for her birthday, Laurie passed away from leukemia. Sometime before she passed, the two of us had a heart-to-heart talk about her illness. I made a vow to her that if she didn't wake up one day, I would live my life for both of us. I have done just that.

In fifth grade, we were assigned desks. Mine was in the back and I had to squint again to try to see the blackboard. Finally, my parents took me to see the Eye Doctor. Upon his exam, we learned that I did indeed need glasses. Glasses were ordered and I was absolutely astounded that I could make out pebbles on top of parking lots. Billboard signs had words on them! I could see blades of grass, leaves on trees, and so much more. I could see the people on TV without walking up close to see them. I had listened to the television programs as though they were radio shows for my entire life. I knew every commercial by heart and was absolutely amazed to actually see the products that were pitched with jingles. A new world was opening for me, and I loved it!

"Bundles of Love" | "I Vant to be Alone"

Family of Origin-Jorgensen: L-R: Robert, Debra Lee, Rick, Shelley, Marlene

Mentor of Origin, Bette Darrell-Davis

CHAPTER 1 PART 2

GOD-GIVEN TALENT LEADS TO ENTERTAINMENT

I know the plans I have for you, says God.
Plans to give you a hope and a future.[1]

Singing and Dancing

THROUGH ALL OF this, my dancing lessons brought me so much joy and relief from the previously disappointing days at school without glasses. As I turned 12, my Dance Teacher, Ms. Bette Darrell, had derived a Performance Act of select dancers to tour various Shriner Hospitals and other health facilities. I was lucky enough to be chosen as one of the Dancers. We performed on Saturdays, and it was the highlight of my life, at that time.

One Saturday, as we were performing, the reel-to-reel tape we performed with broke. We were many in a group. We had no music and needed to stay on rhythm. I started singing the song, which was "Secret Agent". I sang it without dropping a beat, and as loudly as I could. We finished the performance to much applause! After the performance, my Dance Teacher-who had been an old-time professional Vaudevillian, took me aside from the other dancers. She exclaimed, "You are not only a dancer, but you are also a singer". She was determined to make me a nightclub entertainer. We started private lessons. My secret was out and finally, everybody knew I could sing.

This gave me great confidence. Seventh grade was starting soon, and I would be attending our new Junior High School. Try outs for plays at school, meant so much to me. Choir Director, Mr. Pribble, cast me as Dolly Levi in **Hello Dolly**, The Narrator in **Frankie and Johnny**, and Minerva in **Best Foot Forward**.

At thirteen, my first professional "break" came when I auditioned for the "Dick Macko Orchestra and Polka Band". This band was just incredible and is now showcased in the Minnesota Music Hall of Fame. I sang on the weekends all through my teen years. Yes! I did have Chaperones-my parents and grandparents would take turns accompanying me while I sang. My Grandma Isabelle would alter my gowns for singing, and in later years, she'd make outfits, too. When the band took breaks, I'd be in a quiet cloak room doing my homework. I enjoyed watching the Ballroom dancers. These couples would Polka, Waltz, Schottische, Foxtrot, Boogie Woogie, Watusi, and show off every form of the Latin Salsa Boogaloo!! What great training this was for a young vocalist!

Occasionally, I would get the chance to sing with the "Jules Herman Orchestra" and his wife, Miss Lois Best. Both Jules Herman and Lois Best were part of the original Lawrence Welk Orchestra. Miss Best was the original Lawrence Welk Champagne Lady. More incredible training for a 16-year-old.

While in High School, I continued to audition for plays. Mr. Gordon Barry cast me as Fan Tan Fanny in **Flower Drum Song**. Mr. James Olson cast me as Fanny Brice in **Funny Girl** and as play choreographer in **Man of La Mancha**.

When I graduated from High School at 17, I became part of a popular nightclub act called the Edgewater Eight. We performed at the renowned

Edgewater Inn Supper Club located on the bank of the Mississippi River in Northeast Minneapolis. During the daytime, I also took general accredited classes at the University of Minnesota. The Edgewater Inn was managed by Mr. Gil Swenberger. He and his wife, Marty treated me like a daughter. The Swenberger's were kind enough to visit me when I went to college out-of-state. They made a lovely "fuss" over me throughout my career.

Singing with Dick Macko Orchestra in later years.

Nothing better. Home for the Holidays!

Edgewater 8 Reunion, Big Top Chautauqua, Bayfield, Wisconsin

Talking shop with Don Stolz, Old Log Theater-Twin Cities

CHAPTER 1 PART 3

MORE ENTERTAINING
IN COLLEGE

AT AGE 18, I sent out applications to two performance art colleges. I also submitted a cassette tape of my vocal rendition for the song, *"Cabaret"*. Edgewater Eight band leader, Frank Oliveri, accompanied me on Piano for the tape. The two colleges were Julliard in NYC, and School of Performing and Visual Arts at United States International University in San Diego. I was accepted to both colleges, on scholarships. What was I to do?

I decided to attend USIU in San Diego, CA. Why? Well, after growing up in Minnesota and fighting the cold weather for years, it seemed that a warm climate would suit me perfectly. I also liked the idea of being close to Hollywood! After all, movies were my total inspiration.

Thus began my training at the School of Performing and Visual Arts at USIU, in San Diego. The classes were beyond challenging. I studied strict technique in Ballet, Jazz, Tap, and Modern Dance. Our Dance teachers were former MGM Contract Dancers, Jack Tygett and his wife, Marge Tygett, among others. All teachers whipped me into incredible nimbleness. My Drama Teachers were of the highest caliber, having acting credits from the Theater District of NYC. Actor Dennis Turner was the Dialect and Diction Coach. Not only did he train us, but Mr. Turner simultaneously trained movie actors needing to learn an authentic dialect or accent, for roles in Hollywood movies.

My Voice Teachers were Sarah Fleming and Ermen Moradi. Both of my teachers were professional opera singers and had entrancing voices. Because of their strict training, I worked my voice with regimental diligence. My vocal range improved. Both of my teachers thought I should sing Opera. I learned arias in German, French, and Italian. Classical vocal training was giving me a solid foundation for future success and protection of my voice.

Aside from my performance studies, any class in History fascinated me. I also took classes in Piano and Music Theory. Being on Scholarship meant that I had work study hours in the Main Library. I learned how to card catalog and how to keep unruly students quiet and focused on their homework.

We had students from all over the world at our university. I met and became friends with many people that had different customs from my own. This was my first experience in Social Diversity, and I loved it! Learning all about different ways of life and customs different than mine was a true eye opener. I was now dealing with people from all sorts of faiths and backgrounds. People were more open and would discuss Allah. Then we would discuss the Christian ideals. We would all exchange our viewpoints, and everyone got along. It was not like it is today where people are just wanting to destroy somebody who doesn't have their point of view. The information was overwhelming at times, but having been taught that God makes no mistakes, I just rolled with it.

I believed God had me learning about so many different people and their countries for a reason. I especially enjoyed learning new things to do with religious customs from different parts of the world. How was all this information going to fit into my life? Time would eventually reveal the reasons, but for now, I was along for the ride.

While attending USIU, part of the accessible curriculum entailed studying at one of the International Campuses. I chose Mexico City and studied at Universidad de las Americas-USIU. After a year in Mexico City, I had learned to speak and write in Spanish. I explored Latin Heritage and Latin History, focusing on the Mexican American War, and the Spanish

American War. I also took a Literary course that focused on the Bible-King James Version. Also studied was a Literary course on Popol Vuh, the Sacred Book of the Mayans. Once again, I worked in the USIU Library, where I read up on everything to do with Latin culture. Due to my extensive research, I was able to see the world through different eyes. When I grew tired from reading in Spanish, it was it was a relief to read the English Language paper, *The News*. One article I read was about the closing and demolition of the Marigold Ballroom in Minneapolis. I sang there many times; this really broke my heart. I was so far away from home. Yet, *The News* was reaching out to me, as though I was no farther away than the Marigold Ballroom dance floor. After crying a few tears, I shook it off, and went back to card cataloging. It was time to continue my research. I embraced my own traces of Spanish lineage, and life would never be the same.

United States International University was founded by Leland Ghent Stanford, in 1924. Original names for this institution were Balboa Law College, Balboa University and California Western University. In 1953, Dr. William C. Rust became its president. In 1966, Dr. Rust started to transform the university's vision "to create global understanding through a single university with campuses all over the world". In 1968, Dr. Rust changed the college name to United States International University. California Western School of Law remained a part of USIU until 1975.

The college was not for profit, and many Christian Organizations, such as United Methodist Church donated to the world-wide campuses. Dr Rust had a huge vision. Part of the vision was the educational training of people to become managerial key men and key women within various American Corporations throughout the world. A strong belief held within educational and professional training, was acceptance and respect for cultural differences.

Before leaving Minnesota for full-time college, my dad and I traded in my high school vehicle for a new Pontiac Ventura, so I could safely drive across the country. Michele Haskins-Grindal, my best friend from High School, accompanied me on the long trip. My car was so heavily packed, that the tires popped, from the heat, in the middle of the desert. All four tires needed replacement by the time we hit the California border. When we arrived in San Diego, the gas prices were extremely high! America was in the middle of major gas crunch. We all had to stand in line to pump our gas. It could take hours.

Our university not only had students attending classes on scholarships, USIU catered to international students with deep pockets. On weekends, some of the Middle Eastern students would rent penthouses at various luxury Hotels in San Diego or Los Angeles. The partiers would trash the rooms over the weekend. By Monday morning, their parents would have to pay for the damages. The young hosts of the parties didn't think much of it. This pattern for college parties seemed to be a steady occurrence. Celebrating like this was definitely not in my wheelhouse. Was there that much Middle Eastern money to go around? This is when I began to understand the value of Oil. Supply and demand.

I was studying at the School of Performing and Visual Arts. Mornings were all about classes in ballet, jazz, tap, and modern dance. Instructors broke my talent down completely, especially my two voice coaches. My first voice teacher was all about breaking down the voice that I had and starting all over because she wanted to build my range. I felt I wasn't good at singing anymore. My second voice teacher helped me to rebuild my vocal confidence. Maybe I could still sing, after all?

All teachers stripped us of our natural performance habits, whether they were good or bad, and tried to mold us into industry standards of success. My first love was dance. In the first two years, it felt as though I had two left feet. Why was I trying so hard? I just felt that I was going to be a failure. I really did. However, I kept going to school and trying to learn the technical methods being taught.

Experiencing Dinner Theater

I started my Junior Year in College on Scholarship and Work Study, again. I was grateful to have half of my Tuition paid with Scholarship, ¼ paid with Work Study, and ¼ paid with Student Loan, However, I was getting very weary of having no pocket change.

I noticed my friend Susan Sacker was buying herself new clothes and had plenty of gas for her vehicle. She was happy and driving all over San Diego having fun lunches and making friends outside of school. It seemed we weren't hanging out anymore because she was always busy, and she was becoming very confident.

Susan was getting better grades and seemed very focused in class. Our teachers seemed to have more respect for her abilities, also.

One day, she took me out to lunch. I was so curious as to how she was doing all of this with a big grin on her face every day. She seemed so "special." I finally mustered up the courage and asked her how she was managing to accomplish all of this. I asked her what was going on. She then confided in me that she was working as a singing waitress at a brand-new Dinner Theater in Downtown San Diego. One of the waiters was leaving soon and moving to LA. Susan said she would try to get me a closed-door audition at the Theater.

About three days later, she came to me and said, "I got you the audition!"

She was so happy! The following week, I went to the closed call audition and got that job! The two of us started to ride share and perform at night in the "Broadway Toppers" Waiters and Waitresses Show. We, of course, waited on tables, sang our hearts out, and made some tips! Cha-ching! Pocket money appeared!

I could set my singing waitress schedule around my classes and work study. I worked most nights and didn't get home until midnight. Then, I was up for Ballet class at 7 a.m., Monday through Friday. It was an unbearable schedule, but so worth it! The patrons at the Broadway Dinner Theater in Downtown San Diego gave us so much applause! This really helped to boost our confidence! Now, both of us were "Special".

May I add a Total Disclaimer: You can only do this when you are very young! Try at your own discretion and caution...

I just started flourishing again. It seemed that I finally had some people saying, "This girl has got a vocal range. She can dance, act and she can sing. She's great."

Our Dinner Theater also produced Actors Equity Comedy and Musical Theater Plays. We were only 120 miles away from Los Angeles. This meant that we always had well-known actors and actresses in our midst, appearing onstage in the shows, and applauding in the audience. We were a hot spot for talent.

Our directors, producers, costumers, choreographers, and stars of each show were top-notch. All were seasoned professionals with Movie, TV, and Broadway credits to their names. For instance, Nolan Miller designed costumes for "Good, Good Friends", an original musical produced at Broadway Dinner Theater. I was absolutely impressed with their professionalism and work ethic. So much to learn at the theater each night and in rehearsals.

Then, to wake up to classes every day with more sage education from another array of top notch and seasoned professionals?

I was living and breathing in Performance Art Paradise!

By the end of my junior year at USIU-SPVA, I was cast as Hodel in **Fiddler on the Roof** at Broadway Dinner Theater and earned my Actor's Equity Card. I was now a professional working actress, with one more school year left before College Graduation in 1977. Upon graduation I felt that with God I could do anything. What an amazing accomplishment!

Some of the life lessons I garnered during my first season of life from birth through college graduation were...

1.) Get yourself a college, trade school or military education. You will always be employed, with possibility of advancement, if you have educational training beyond your high school diploma. You will be able to stand out from the other applicants.

2.) Your self-esteem can depend upon the amount of training you give yourself. Never underestimate the power of learning. To be successful, you must be open to new ideas for the rest of your life. Think of learning as the greatest gift you can give to yourself. Expand your mind. Expand your horizons.

3.) When you feel like giving up, say to yourself, "let me sleep on it", "let me pray on it". Always ask God for guidance in all things. Remember that every experience can lead to a breakthrough for you.

4.) If you fail in something, welcome to the club! Failure will teach you where you need to improve and lead you to your successes. Believe in yourself and never give up!

In *Grit: The Power of Passion and Perseverance*, Dr. Angela Duckworth writes,

> *Follow your passion* is a popular theme of commencement speeches. I've sat through my fair share, both as a student and professor. I'd wager that at least half of all speakers, maybe more, underscore the importance of doing something you love. *[And I was doing just that…entertaining, dancing and singing were my passion.]*

For instance, Will Shortz, long-time editor of the *New York Times* crossword puzzle, told students at Indiana University: "My advice for you is, figure out what you enjoy doing most in life, and then try to do it full-time. Life is short. Follow your passion."[2]

I discovered in my first season of life that…

- God made me special, unique, with talents and gifts in music, dance, and entertaining others.
- More than being talented and gifted, I had a passion, and love for entertaining, singing and dancing.
- Even more, I needed to work hard and practice a lot, to get better and create opportunities for fulfilling my passionate dreams.
- Faith, Family, and Friends were important anchors of support for my confidence and strength to persevere through any hardships or disappointments I would face.

More growth was to come for me. A person never stops learning. I encourage you to learn from these life lessons I experienced.

Ask Yourself…

- *Do you believe that God made you special and have good plans for your future?* Read Psalm 139 and Jeremiah 29:11
- *What are you passionate about? What are you doing to pursue your passion?*
- *When you face hardships and disappointments, are you persevering? If not, who will you turn to for help and support?*

Know Who You Are

For we are God's masterpiece.
He has created us anew in Christ Jesus,
so we can do the good things he planned for us long ago.
(Ephesians 2:10)

Everyone has his own specific vocation or mission in life;
everyone must carry out a concrete assignment that demands fulfillment.
Therein he cannot be replaced, nor can his life be repeated,
thus, everyone's task is unique as his specific opportunity to implement it.
-Viktor E. Frankl

"For I know the plans I have for you," says the Lord. They are plans for
good and not for disaster, to give you a future and a hope."
(Jeremiah 29:11)

DISCOVERING AND GROWING MY INNER SELF-IDENTITY

I had my first Charismatic Spiritual Conversion in 1976-77 while on the road, performing in the Broadway International Spotlight Tour for "A Little Night Music."

> **God had always been my number one.**
> **I loved God, loved others as I loved myself.**
> **He was my confidence and my strength.**
> **I always knew I couldn't do anything without God**
> **in my life**.

I was struggling with the character of Petra, my part in *A Little Night Music*. Petra had very loose morals. I needed God's permission to play this part to the fullest. I was in no way mirrored to this character. Our cast, crew and orchestra had just finished up our rehearsals on a Broadway sound stage, near Times Square. We had performed for Stephen Sondheim, Hal Prince and other well-known musical theater originators. Everyone seemed pleased with our remake of their show.

We headed out to begin our tour the next day. We gave our tour's first performance at one of the east coast Ivy League Schools. We were at the start of a sixty-seven-city tour of the United States and Canada. I was trying to reconcile myself with this role. I did the role, but it was a mechanical performance. I was doing what they directed within the blocking. What was expected of me. I sang it well. However, the Broadway Spotlight Series Producer, Mr. Gordon Crowe, wasn't very excited about me, because he didn't think my body was "zaftig" enough to do the role. He said this right in front of me, (in a much more unrefined way)….

Our Director, Mr. John Bowab, reassured Mr. Gordon Crowe. "Just let her get into the role, she's going to be fine.", said Mr. Bowab. Honestly, I was not very happy with what I was doing, at the beginning, either. I didn't believe I was ever going to be fine. I wasn't a standout, yet.

That night, after our first performance, I couldn't sleep. Afraid that I might wake up my roommate, I decided to go into the bathroom to pray about how I was going to get this role under my belt. Suddenly, it was as though an electrical current raced and raged through my body. Oh, my gosh! It was like lightning! It was a soul conversion! I started to speak in tongues! I was so excited that I woke up my roommate to tell her all about my "Good News". Waking her up to share what was going on with me, scared her half to death!

Unfortunately, the rest of the cast heard about my conversion, and they thought I had a nervous breakdown. From then on, the cast treated me as though I was emotionally unstable. What a cross to bear when on the road in small quarters. I spent a great deal of my down time regretting my decision to open my mouth about my conversion experience to someone in the cast. I became socially misunderstood.

However, my "born again" experience proved that my life was redeemed by Jesus. I would never be the same again. I was a new creature in Christ. I sang and acted my heart out, and in time, became the breakout actress and singing character of the show. The applause and cheers at Curtain Calls became a nightly occurrence. I hit my stride as an actress, and never looked back.

My cast-mates continued to ridicule me, but I didn't let it into my heart. I was a child of God playing the role of a person only God could understand and continue to love. Petra was ostracized and so was I. We became one in the eyes of God.

I kept remembering a biblical Psalm (139) that told me I was a child of God, wondrously made, dearly beloved, and precious in His sight. I wasn't searching for my identity…I knew who I was. My goal in all I did wasn't to please others, but simply to please God and be true to myself. I trusted my *gut*. I read somewhere that one's gut was "**G**od's **U**ltimate **T**ruth." How true that was to become for me.

When the Tour was over, I went back to USIU in San Diego, finished out my classes, my credits, and continued to work at Broadway Dinner Theater. I then graduated with my BA in Music and Voice, in the Spring of 1977.

During my senior year, Director and Producer Don Wortman, from the Broadway Dinner Theater, went to my school to conduct a seminar. Mr. Wortman told the students "Out of all the young people I've been working with, Debbie could become 'a major star'". "If she continues to listen and learn, she's got the talent to go far in this business." I was unaware of what he had said. Fellow classmates told me about this later, that summer. This assessment was extremely humbling. How does a person try to live up to the comments expressed by someone like Mr. Don Wortman?

CHAPTER 2 PART 2

THE AUDITION

THE NEXT ARTISTIC highlight of my life was being cast in *Lido de Paris* at the fabulous Stardust Hotel and Casino, in Las Vegas. Winning the principal singing role in *Lido de Paris* wasn't easy…My casting was not by chance, but by my own determination.

While continuing to work at the Broadway Dinner Theater, one of the cast members of *Pal Joey* (a musical in which I was playing the part of Linda English), thought we all should go to Las Vegas, as we had a few days off. The idea was to audition for *Lido de Paris* at the Stardust Hotel and Casino. At that time, I had a little Honda Civic, and we piled into my car to drive to Las Vegas. We were halfway there and stopped at a coffee shop, along the way. While having a snack and sipping our coffee, somebody pulled out the audition ad that was posted in Variety. Variety is the entertainment resource for news and views.

The Audition Open Call clearly stated that the minimum height requirement for all female performers was 5'8". I am 5'4" tall. With reality about the audition sinking in, I continued to drive everyone to Las Vegas, anyway. Within my private thoughts, I knew that I was cheeky enough to make myself heard at that audition.

The sun was going down as we continued our journey through the desert. As the sky was growing darker, ahead of us on the horizon, was a blinding vision of light. We were driving toward that light! The vision appeared to be a spotlight upon the landscape, peering down from the sky above!

I fixed my eyes on the road ahead. As we approached what seemed to be a transparent gate, or a portal out of the darkness, we could see multitudes of neon colors! To me, it looked as though it might be Heaven!

I gripped the steering wheel and held my breath…Right smack dab in front of us, was a very conspicuously placed and well-lit sign. The sign simply exclaimed, WELCOME TO FABULOUS LAS VEGAS, NEVADA!

We were in awe! We drove down the Las Vegas Strip in amazement! The traffic was very slow. All vehicles were admiring the displays of colorful neon lights splashed on both sides of the road. As we slowly veered along, we were bumper to bumper. Our tired eyes settled upon a beautifully refined, flickering array of colors to the left. While rolling toward an up-close view, we could see that this was the Stardust Marquee!

We were mesmerized. We smoothly yielded our way into the Stardust parking lot. We then walked into the Stardust Casino. Once inside, we were fascinated by what we saw! Right then and there, I made a secret pact to myself to become a part of Las Vegas. This Ultimate Glittering Jewel in the Mojave Desert. The Entertainment Capitol of the World!

The next day was the Audition Open Call. A well-dressed and well-groomed gentleman was in charge. I found out that he was Mr. Donn Arden, the legendary Producer and Director. He was nicknamed the "Master of Disaster" for his special effects staging, such as the sinking of the Titanic. His work was influenced by Busby Berkley and Florence Ziegfeld.

I listened to what seemed to be countless singers competing for the lead roles. I assessed my odds, trying to muster my inner courage. When I did try to audition, Mr. Donn Arden cut me right away. He refused to hear me sing. I didn't fit his advertised criteria.

As I watched my friends audition, I found new determination and inspiration. Incredibly, two of my road trip companions were asked to come back a few days later, for a second vocal audition. As their names were read from the Callback list, I decided to step up, and ask for one more chance. I like fairness and was going to make sure that I got something out of this trip…

I approached Mr. Donn Arden, asking him if he truly wanted to see my friends audition again. He answered, "Yes." With my knees shaking, I struck a bargain with him, saying, "Well, you'll need to see me too, because I'm their ride home." After half-chuckling to himself, Mr. Arden looked me squarely in the face. He said, "Young lady, you are a very clever girl. You have won your token singing audition at Callbacks". He then announced over his cordless microphone that I was to be "The Token Singer" at Callbacks, as it was my job to chauffeur the other singers back to San Diego.

When Callback Day finally rolled around, my funds were depleted. After all, I had spent my money on places to stay in Las Vegas. I was financially broke, with ten dollars left to my name. Adelaide Robbins, a phenomenal piano player, had been individually hired by most of the auditioners to better showcase their voices. I begged her to play for me and gave her my last ten dollars.

At the end of the Callback process, true to his word, Mr. Donn Arden called me up to the stage. He again announced me as "The Token Singer". I started to sing. Adelaide Robbins followed my lead.

We began with *Everything's Coming Up Roses*. Mr. Donn Arden was tickled! He started calling out commands. "Stop! Sing- *Somewhere Over the Rainbow*!". "Stop! Sing- *The Trolley Song*!". "Stop! Sing- *O Mio Babbino Caro*!". "Stop-NOW, DANCE!" … "Show me a triple pirouette!". "Now, show me a Triple Time Step!". "Now, Jete and Chaine turn all across the stage!". "Now, show me Tour Jete with Pirouettes-as many in a row, as you can do!!".

I danced all over the stage, doing everything that he asked me to do. Mr. Donn Arden then proclaimed, "Young lady, you just got yourself a

Lead in my new show! Listen, everybody, it doesn't matter if she is too short! The Lead is her position!!".

Of course, the pre-cast members of the show whispered among themselves that I must have a lot of "Juice" to win the part. I found out later that "Juice" meant I had Mafia support. Ha! I laughed to myself because my "Juice" was God-Given and Driven! I won that audition fair and square…

Being the only singer in the show with height below the height requirement meant that the costume makers in Paris had to disguise my stature. They had to customize and build up my shoes to the height of the other performers. The platform shoes I wore were at least three inches high! While performing, I had to stylishly walk or run up and down 30-foot staircases, but I was so young, I didn't care. That was how my life was!

Being contracted as a Principal Singer meant that you worked without a night or day off for six months. Two shows per night with three shows on Saturday. After six months, it was time for three days off. After three days, I came back to work, and the cycle would begin again. This was a grueling schedule, but oh, so worth it! A consummate entertainer lives for the stage, the cast, the crew, the orchestra, the spotlights and the crowd. I was no exception.

Stardust Marquee-Lido de Paris Twelfth Edition, "Allez Lido"

ACT I: Paris Toujours! Toujours Lido! Section of: Bluebells, Arden-Kelly Boy Dancers and Singers, and me Cashman Photography

Debra Lee Kristian with Arden-Kelly Boy Singers **Scene 4. Chanson d'Amour** *"Let's Fall in Love", "S'Wonderful"* Cashman Photography

Debra Lee Kristian- Publicity Photo Larry Hannah Photography

ACT lll. Le Jardin de Versailles Scene 3. Le Carnaval de Venise Scene 1. "Opera *Aria de Versailles*" All Live Photos: ABCDVDVIDEO

The Loves of Casanova Gondolas on Grand Canal
"Opera *Aria Pio Mi*-Canalazzo Venezia" Cashman Photography

ACT Vll. Les Rues de Paris, Champs Elysees, All Live Photos: ABCDVIDEO

Scene 2. Place Vendome, Arc de Triomphe

"Avec"

Scene 5. Rue Royale | Chez Maxim

"Fascination" Duet Debra Lee Kristian and Carl Lindstrom

Original Cast, *"**Allez Lido** "*

GRAND FINALE-Act IX. *"Bonsoir, A Bientot"* | *"Allez Lido"*

"Paris Je T'Aime"

CHAPTER 3 PART 1

LAS VEGAS – 24/7 GLITZ, GAMING AND GRIT

ONE OF THE highlights of preparation for my singing role in Lido de Paris was the invitation to rehearse with Mr. Donn Arden and staff at his offices, located at the MGM Studios in Culver City. Imagine driving through the Vintage MGM Studio Gates and being greeted by security upon entering! This was so surreal-my dreams were coming true! During rehearsal, Mr. Arden showed me sketches and swatches of fabrics for the beautiful costumes that I would soon be wearing. After the singing rehearsals, there was a meal in the MGM Commissary. I noticed working actors, actresses and various other studio employees were also having their noon lunch. Could it get any better than this?

The full cast rehearsals for the ***Lido de Paris*** show began sometime in the Summer of 1977. What can you do, when you feel like you stick out like a sore thumb? Everyone was so very tall! The only saving grace was knowing that all my shoes were being custom made to make me appear taller. My castmates were also doubtful about my appearance in the show. However, they knew nothing of the secret weapons being fashioned for me. Wonderful, custom designed, and color blocked platform shoes in every color, to disguise my height.

That Summer in August, Elvis died. The entire Las Vegas Entertainment and Tourism community was broken hearted. Some of the people involved with our show had known him or had worked with him. Everyone will never forget how sad the entire town of Las Vegas was during this time. People all over the city were sobbing, and grief stricken. Elvis always knew that Jesus Christ was The King of Kings. Elvis did so much for so many, in the name of Jesus. Elvis will always be remembered as The King of Rock and Roll.

The show finally opened right before the Holidays. All our costumes, headpieces, feathers, shoes, jewelry, and hair pieces were custom made. They were shipped in from Europe. I was wearing several $4000 gowns, worth approximately $20,000, per gown, by today's standards. We had nothing but the very best. No imitations allowed. I was dripping in what I was told to be Swarovski Jewels, Swarovski Rhinestones, imported feathers, furs, and fabulous silks. Our audiences were filled with all the A-List Celebrities of the day! The A-Listers were ushered backstage after the shows, and we met them all!

One of the A-Listers was Valerie Perrine. She had been a Stardust **Lido de Paris** Showgirl, earlier in her career. She came into our dressing room, and asked if she could sit in my chair. Of course, I got out the chair, so she could sit down. Valerie then sat down, waited a beat, and said, "I always wanted to sit here". What a compliment that was!

Onstage, I appeared tall and exotic. Backstage was another story. I was still too short. My nickname was "The Midget." The song, "Short People" by Randy Newman, was the comic relief mantra backstage.

I was also chided by several key Stardust Executives. Our Entertainment Director-Food and Beverage Manager was Mr. Frank Rosenthal. It was common knowledge that Mr. Rosenthal ran the entire Stardust Casino. The rumors were that the Nevada Gaming Commission probably would not grant Mr. Rosenthal the coveted Gaming License to legitimately run any casino in Nevada. Thus, he took on various titles within the hierarchy of the Stardust Hotel and Casino, in order to be able to run the entire operation.

Mr. Rosenthal was very particular about our show and the people in our show. Mr. Rosenthal had his pulse on everything concerning the Stardust Hotel and Casino. Also, the rumors were that he ran other gambling establishments along the Las Vegas Strip as well as Downtown Las Vegas.

Of course, there were many rumors backstage about his management style. One thing you never wanted to have happen to you, was to be summoned to answer a phone call backstage, on "The Red Phone". "The Red Phone" was rumored to be your dismissal. On the other hand, it also could mean your promotion. Regardless, this was a cringeworthy signal, and we all prayed to be absolved of "The Red Phone" method, for backstage communication.

Mr. Rosenthal seemed to appreciate my talent, but it was whispered that my height was a real issue for him. When he finally came to resolve that I wasn't going to grow any taller, he nicknamed me, "Seabiscuit". This, of course was a compliment, but I told him that I was not a biscuit, I was a human being.

Little did I realize what a compliment he was giving me. How could I have knowledge about horse racing? How could I have known who "Seabiscuit" was? The true "Seabiscuit" was a champion racehorse that didn't fit the racehorse image. "Seabiscuit" was a winner to beat every odd against him. The horse loved to race and was all heart. Mr. Rosenthal, a genius Odds-maker within the world of Sports, knew his craft. He understood my passion was to be the best, regardless of any stereotype or prejudice. My job was to win over the sold-out audience, night after night.

About three months into the opening of our show, my responsibilities grew from five musical singing spots into ten. The other Female Principal Singer took another job. Mr. Rosenthal then contracted me to perform every female singing spot within *Lido de Paris*, at the Stardust. This change was very demanding, but I loved it! Being less tall than the others didn't matter as much, anymore. I could wrap myself around all the female singing parts, right in the center of the stage. All the height comparisons would be less noticeable.

One more tidbit for you-the premise for the hit movie, **Casino**, is an adaptation from the book, ***Casino-Love and Honor in Las Vegas***, written by Nicholas Pileggi. **Casino** is an adapted portrayal of the life and times of Mr. Frank Rosenthal, and the people who were part of it. There was a time when Mr. Rosenthal said that he was going to be writing a movie about his life within the Las Vegas casino industry. Mr. Rosenthal went so far as to say that Robert DeNiro would play him in the movie about his life. The backstage area of **Lido de Paris** was a haven for rumor, disparaging inuendo, and truth. Some of our cast members laughed at this assertion. However, Mr. Rosenthal was right, God rest his soul.

A good thing to come out of my fight to perform in a Las Vegas Extravaganza with such a stringent height requirement, is that my personal experience helped to change the system. Finally, other talented singers would be able to audition and be cast in Las Vegas Extravaganzas, regardless of how tall they were. This became the wave of the future for Las Vegas Revue Vocalists. Of course, all had custom made shoes to disguise their true stature. I was very pleased to see this change and to witness the results, when I watched the show, **Jubilee** right before it closed in 2016. Coincidentally, this was the last remnant of the Donn Arden Production Shows. May Mr. Donn Arden rest in peace. His keen theatrical eye created legendary shows that will never be forgotten.

To think that my casting and camouflaged shoes might have been a prototype to open the doors and break through the height requirement for singers, in Las Vegas Production Shows, is truly amazing. Mr. Donn Arden paved the way for me to be a Principal Singer in one of his Extravaganzas. Believe me, I paid the dues for my participation with two shows Sunday through Friday, and three shows on Saturday. This went on for six months straight, three days off for a vacation, then return to do it all over again. Wash-Rinse-Repeat…

I discovered that my passion for entertaining plus my relentless practice and perseverance made others take notice of me. My work ethic opened so many doors for exciting opportunities. One of the developing themes for living my life to the max, (and for living yours as well), is BE GRITTY.

"Grit is not just simple elbow-grease term for rugged persistence. It is an often-invisible display of endurance that lets you stay in an uncomfortable place, work hard to improve upon a given interest, and do it again and again."

— Sarah Lewis[3]

Angela Duckworth, Ph.D., as a behavioral psychologist, researched how athletes, artists, business leaders, cultural icons, and successful people from numerous walks of life rose to the top in their fields through...

- *passionate interest,*
- *indomitable practice,*
- *focused purpose, and*
- *indefatigable hope.*

While some were highly intelligent or "over the moon" gifted in their talents and skills, many were simply good or even average at their artistry, sport, or profession. Their winning success came about through *grit* which she detailed in her bestselling book, *Grit: The Power of Passion and Perseverance.*

It is a joy to share insights from Dr. Duckworth within my story. However, let me say upfront that grit isn't everything needed to overcome all the physical, psychological, and spiritual challenges in my life or yours.

As Duckworth adds,

So, grit isn't everything. There are many other things a person needs in order to grow and flourish. Character is plural.
One way to think about grit is to understand how it relates to other aspects of character. In assessing grit along with other virtues, I find three reliable clusters. I refer to them as the intrapersonal, interpersonal, and intellectual dimensions of character. You could also call them strengths of will, heart, and mind.[4]

My gritty mantra throughout each season of my life has been…

Mind over Matter!

This requires discipline and self-control. Your mind can choose to take control. You discover the value of being proactive instead of reactive, positive not negative…

> hopeful instead of despairing…
> reality-based instead of fantasizing…
> seizing the moment while avoiding procrastination…
> taking responsibility for your decisions…
> and most of all, believing your hope and strength come from God.

> **Stop wearing your Wishbone where your Backbone ought to be…**

> **- Elizabeth Gilbert**

CHAPTER 3 PART 2

DANGEROUS TIMES

THERE WERE TIMES at the Stardust, when I was very worried for my well-being. I felt at times like the singing canary that the cat wanted to devour. I didn't much care for the game. I was worried about the repercussions. The pressure seemed tremendous. One evening after our shows, I was with my friends in the Starlight Lounge listening to the music. I was interrupted by Mr. Rosenthal with a directive to go to the entrance of the Stardust and start his car. He handed me his keys and sent me on my way. At the entrance to the Casino, I naively asked the Valet, "Which car belongs to Mr. Rosenthal?" … The keys were abruptly grabbed from my hand, and I was scolded to NEVER TRY TO START Mr. Rosenthal's CAR AGAIN! I found out later that Mr. Rosenthal was always afraid that his car might be blown up. Eventually, it was.

When you work and live in Las Vegas, you will usually run into old friends, teachers and of course, family members more often than you would living in any other city. Everyone loves Las Vegas! I saw so many people and had frequent visitors from Minnesota, and North Dakota. Of course, my favorite visitor from North Dakota was my Grandpa Phil Ell. My grandfather was a tried-and-true cowboy. When he was young, Grandpa was a bucking bronco competitor in northwestern rodeos. He had a farm where he raised specialty horses, and greyhounds for Florida racing. He owned a tri-state salvage business and land with mineral rights.

Obviously, Grandpa loved risk, and when he walked into the Stardust, he was dressed in his western wear best. He wore a 10-gallon white Stetson, and a suit to match. He flashed a lot of cash at the tables and made sure all of the dealers and pit bosses knew who he was. He also made sure everyone on the casino floor knew how important I was, to him. He always called me "City-Slicker", and wasn't about to stop, just because I was in "some big, fancy show". I think we may have brought humor to the pit that weekend. I honestly felt the pressure loosen up the weekend he came to town. We had a grand time together.

My mother and sister came to see me in *Lido de Paris,* when the show first opened. My sister was 5'9'. When I introduced mom and Shelley to Mr. Rosenthal, he offered my sister a spot in the show right then and there! She was still in High School and of course, politely declined.

My dad was in Las Vegas a few times, while I was in the *Lido de Paris*, but he usually stayed at the MGM. His trips to town were for conventions in advertising and marketing. One weekend, when he was bringing my stepmom along, they decided to stay at the Stardust. They came to see the show together. The three of us went into the Starlight Lounge after my second show, but my stepmom decided to head off to the hotel room before my dad.

Dad and I continued to watch the lounge acts, and chat about our family and my career. As we continued our conversation, the Executives and Mr. Rosenthal took a table very close to us in the lounge. They sat down with irritated looks on their faces. Instead of watching the lounge acts, they were watching us. I could sense acrimony within their body language and the acrimony was directed at my dad and me. My dad could sense it, too. We decided to approach their table, so my dad could be introduced.

Upon meeting my dad, the Executives almost fell out of their chairs with relief and laughter. Mr. Rosenthal said that he thought my dad was way too young to be my father. Mr. Rosenthal thought my dad was some sort of con man trying to either steal me away from the show or make the moves on me. Mr. Rosenthal then had to quickly cancel the plans he had already put in place to "rough-up" my father, so that my dad would never dream of coming back to the Stardust.

One evening in my dressing room, I found the tiniest little microphone sitting in the curls of one of my seldom used headpieces. I expressed in wonder, where could such a tiny microphone come from? It is so darling! There was also one in a floral arrangement that had just been sent to the dressing room. I commented about the darling mini microphones in the dressing room that I shared with our Lead Adagio Dancer. I believed the mini microphones to be thoughtful decorations. Our Lead Adagio Dancer put her left hand on my shoulder. She held her right hand index finger up to her lips as if to say, "Shush!". She then whispered into my ear, "We are being bugged! Somebody has our dressing room under surveillance!".

This news crushed me. Who is listening to the dressing room conversation? Fearful paranoia took over my body! I couldn't sleep or eat. After this experience, my life just went from day to day. Show to show. As a person, there was no fun-filled existence. My confidence eroded. Who was after us? This overwhelming feeling of mistrust just came over me. Were the Executives listening in on our conversations? Were their friends listening in? Could it be Law Enforcement? I grew more and more paranoid every day.

This is about the time that my grandparents from Minnesota came to my rescue. Both of them took a trip to Las Vegas to visit me. They had just retired after owning a popular bar and restaurant, for many years, in the resort area of Northern Minnesota. My grandparents were staying at my apartment with me. What a relief to have them so close! My grandparents could see how the backstage intrigue, coupled with casino pressure, was affecting me. They were both worried about my safety.

One evening, my grandfather took me aside right before I left for work. This was the same night that he and my grandmother were going to see the show. Grandpa had some surprising news for me. He said, "You go in to work tonight and you tell these people that your grandmother and I will be in the audience". You also tell them, "Back in the day, your grandfather was a rum runner". You tell them, "With all due respect, my grandfather is asking, can you please lighten up?"

I was stunned by what Grandpa had to say. I went to work. As was usually the case, some of the Executives and their friends were hanging around backstage. I greeted them and politely told them what my grandfather said. They stared at me, thunderstruck. After that conversation, it seemed as though many became my protectors.

There was a time for me backstage and onstage when it was reported to me to remedy every little flaw, actual or imagined. My looks seemed to be a major issue for Mr. Rosenthal. He was upset about my height, color of my hair, color of my lipstick, color of my eyes-everything about me, was annoying him. This is when the two Spilotro brothers, Anthony and Michael, came to pay me a visit, at the backstage entrance. Mr. Anthony Spilotro was dismayed about Mr. Rosenthal's current perception of me. Both brothers, not much taller than I am, were concerned. They wanted to know how I was doing. The brothers offered to "have a talk with Mr. Rosenthal." I kept my head about me. I just smiled and said that everything was good. Secretly, I will never forget how grateful I was for that visit! It seemed that all of the complaints went away for a while. May both brothers rest in peace.

Budd Friedman had started another West Coast Improv Comedy Club in Las Vegas. To unwind after work, I would sing at the Comedy Club, right around one o'clock in the morning. Mr. Friedman had orchestrated a Showcase for me on a Friday night. The Showcase would be in the wee hours of the morning, after my shift in Lido de Paris, at the Stardust.

The night before the Showcase, I took my call on the dreaded Red Phone. Mr. Rosenthal was piping mad that I was going to perform a Showcase at the Improv Comedy Club. He angrily ended my performances **at Lido de Paris**. I countered on the Red Phone, "Oh Mr. Rosenthal, I still have one more show to do tonight." With that, he hung up on me. After the second show, I quickly packed up my belongings and left. I was still under contract, but none of this mattered. Mr. Rosenthal considered me insubordinate.

The next morning, as I was supposed to be preparing for the Improv Showcase, I froze. I was so worried about the repercussions from the warnings already shouted out by Mr. Rosenthal, from the night before. I called Budd Friedman to cancel the Showcase. Mr. Friedman tried to convince me to do the show, anyway.

How could I see my way around the threats passed down by Mr. Rosenthal? Were the threats real, or idle? I was too shaken to find out…I reluctantly cancelled and did not show my face at the Improv that night, or any other night. Little did I know that Mr. Budd Friedman had invited some key producers to see me-one of them rumored to be Lorne Michaels, from SNL. Years later, when I tried to contact Friedman, his doors were definitely closed….

You may be wondering…How could the Stardust find a Lead Singer on such short notice? Very easily, as vacation and safety vocal tracks had initially been recorded, should tapes be needed. This way, the show could continue without a live voice. One of the leading dancers had rehearsed all my choreography and learned to lip-synch to my singing. Originally, this was the plan, so that I was able to take a three-day vacation-every six months. When I permanently left, this became the permanent plan.

My safety vocal tracks were part of the show for years to come. In the early eighties, I went to see the show again. The distinct sound of my voice filled the stage. You may ask, was this upsetting to me? Not at all! I was proud that my voice had stood the test of time, beyond my personal performance. At one point, during the eighties, I did receive a small stipend for the unfinished contract and the use of my vocals. For me, at that time in my life, it was not about money. It was about the reassurance of my artistry. My voice had not been replaced. Eventually, some new voice tracks were recorded. However, you could still hear my voice within two scenes of the show.

As sad as it was to leave the Stardust, I knew I was landing on my feet. I had just auditioned for ***Anything Goes*** at the Union Plaza, in Downtown Las Vegas. I was in negotiation for the role of Hope Harcourt. Our Producer was Maynard Sloate. Our Director was Jack Bunch. The musical play was just ideal for me at the time. We had a marvelous, star-studded cast. We played to sold out audiences every night. Finally, I was enjoying my life in Las Vegas and felt no undue pressure while performing at the Union Plaza.

Of course, the word travels fast in Las Vegas. Even more so, when it was a much smaller town. Rumors were flying regarding many misdeeds taking place at the Stardust, within the ranks of the Casino. During that time, I received a phone call from my father, back in Minnesota. Dad had heard legitimate information about a law enforcement bust that might be happening soon, in Las Vegas. He thought it was best for me to leave Las Vegas, for a while. When **Anything Goes** came to an end, I started to look for opportunities elsewhere.

"No is a complete sentence."
-Anne Lamont

Setting healthy boundaries in your relationships and career is one of the most important things you can do. I discovered that I could advance my career and keep my personal boundaries intact even in the entertainment industry. When I said "no" to job offers, or to sexual advances, at times I lost money and professional promotion, but I never lost my sense of self-respect and integrity.

How Not to Make It In Show Business

Bill Murray was about to hire me to be in his new movie. A movie called "Caddy Shack". I auditioned for him in San Diego. He appreciated a printed brochure that I gave him. The brochure publicized me as a singing showgirl, actress and dancer.

Mr. Murray called me at home to say that he was writing a part for me, in the movie. A part for me as 'the Call Girl". "What was a Call Girl?", I asked him. He answered, "Prostitute". "No thanks", I said. He was flabbergasted, "Are you sure?". "Yes", I said. Mr. Murray said, "Really? I'm writing it for you!".

"Not a good idea for me.", I said. (I didn't want to play any sort of prostitute! What would my family think?) … So, Mr. Murray and I exchanged a few more pleasantries, and hung up… Little did I know he was writing a COMEDY! I am a Comedienne! This could have been a great break for me, but I missed it! I could have been featured in one of the CLASSIC MOVIES of ALL TIME! UFF DA!

CHAPTER 4 PART1

BEYOND VEGAS

THE LATIN CONNECTION. The next season of my life is all about my career South of the Border and in the Caribbean. Pat Merl, a dancer and my former Company Manager at Lido de Paris, had left her position at the Stardust to work with Miller-Reich Productions located in Miami, Florida. Pat had hoped to hire me for Cal Neva Lodge in Lake Tahoe, but I was unavailable.

I had taken a contract in Mexico City, to perform for agent Bernard Meder. Mr. Meder was a former Company Manager for Follies Bergère. He had an opening singing position with a new band being formed by previous members of the well-known Latin band, "La Tierra". He immediately put me into their new band, "Luceros Blancos." I stayed in Mexico for a while and had many wonderful opportunities. We recorded a song for RCA-Mexico Records, "Born to Be Alive" which was very popular at the time. We recorded it in Spanish and released it as "Nacio para Vivir".

While performing at Hotel Chapultepec located in the Zona Rosa, I met other entertainers such as Nancy Wilson, along with her amazing piano player, Michael Wolff. When I met Clive Davis, his associate gave me an Arista business card that said, "Let's press you to vinyl." I didn't even understand what "vinyl" meant! Of course, I accidentally misplaced the card. If the card had said, "Let's make a record" or "record a tape," I would have been over the moon! I would have jumped at the chance!

Upon leaving Mexico, it was time to go home to see my family. I was also contemplating a change in lifestyle with a change in career. I needed a new lease on life. It was so good be home with my family and friends. Nothing could replace home.

That is when Pat Merl called me again, about the job at the Cal Neva Lodge in Lake Tahoe. She needed a replacement for the current singer. I just had to turn her down. I needed personal restoration, and family at my side.

The next day, I heard from her boss, Producer Leonard Miller. Mr. Miller tried to convince me to go to Lake Tahoe. His wife, the fabulous Glenda Grainger, was the singer in the show at Cal Neva Lodge. He wanted his wife to come home…Once again, I declined. He then offered to bring me to Puerto Rico in an all-new Extravaganza at the El San Juan Hotel in Puerto Rico. Pat Merl was to go along, as our Company Manager. After some cajoling, I decided to sign the contract and go to San Juan.

What a beautiful and luxurious hotel awaited in San Juan! The El San Juan Hotel and Casino is in a class of its own! Our show was held in the famed Club Tropicoro Showroom. Our cast performed the show six nights a week, with two shows per night. We had Sundays off. This made me very happy, as church could now be a part of my Sunday mornings!

Being bilingual, there were many major breaks for me in San Juan. Young and Rubicam hired me for bilingual voice-over work. I was cast in television commercials as 'La Chica de Chardon"- The Chardon Jeans Girl. There were magazine covers and newspaper articles. During this time, Latin TV Impresario, Sr. Luis Vigoreaux, heard about me through Miller Reich Productions. He invited me to become a recurring Guest Star on his weekly Variety Show, **"Luis Vigoreaux Presenta".** My job on television was to sing and dance. Also portray characters in the skits within his shows. The **"Luis Vigoreaux Presenta"** weekly program was broadcast all over the Caribbean, in Miami, and in NYC. Wherever there was a large Latino population.

Singing and speaking in English and Spanish was such fun! Little Ricky Martin, then the youngest member of the popular Latin boy band,

"Menudo", would sit with me in my dressing room at WAPA 4. Ricky enjoyed watching me put on my makeup and listening to me warm up my voice. He was so curious about other performers. His work ethic was already a prominent feature of his character.

Somewhere within my Puerto Rican journey, I learned firsthand about the "Me Too Movement." I was assaulted by one of the best-known American Icons of that era. He was a household name throughout the world.

We had a cast celebration late into the evening for our visiting Mainland Guest and for his entourage. He prayed The Lord's Prayer in front of the gathering audience and our cast. Pat Merl asked him to walk me home from the El San Juan Hotel, to my beachside condominium. It was very late at night and at that time, women should not be out on the streets and especially not on the beach. That was why I needed an escort home. That evening he assaulted me. This Icon. This Hero. He was nothing but a brute and a coward.

Years later, before this abuser died, I remembered the incident. I felt a spiritual plea to forgive him, but I just couldn't do it. The Lord did not let me get sleep until I promised, "I forgive him." Over the next few days when his death was all over the news, I began to feel the power and release that forgiveness can bring over past abuse. I also reflected on how I had strived to heal my pain by learning Self Defense and Martial Arts while still under contract, in Puerto Rico.

BACK TO THE MAINLAND, AND BEYOND!!

TWO YEARS LATER, as I was enjoying my life in Puerto Rico, Miller Reich Productions decided to send me to Valley Forge for a show being created in a new theater, Lillie Langtry's at Sheraton Valley Forge. Off I went to the Philadelphia area to perform in this new show. After finishing two contracts with Miller Reich Productions at the Sheraton Valley Forge, I began singing at venues located in Downtown Philadelphia.

Next came the Hotel and Casinos in Puerto Rico, Atlantic City, Reno, Laughlin, and of course, Las Vegas. I was part of a Nightclub Duo and Trio while developing my own act. Once my own act was developed, I became a "Fly-On Headliner". To be a "Fly On" act, you would be privately flown to various ports, and set sail on a Cruise Ship as the Headlining Entertainer for a night at sea. Once you would reach the next port, you were privately flown back to the Mainland in order to catch another ship, about to set sail. I began to tour as a "Fly-On" for NCL Ships. Also had great times aboard RCL ships, now known as Disney Cruise Lines. On land, I performed my act at Shoreham Hotel in Washington D.C., and other Showrooms.

Eventually, I started singing at least 6 months out of the year in Las Vegas at Sahara Hotel and Casino, The Dunes Hotel and Casino, Hacienda Hotel and Casino, and in Laughlin, at Harrah's Del Rio Hotel and Casino. This made it possible to go back to Los Angeles where I sang the other remaining months of the year at Windows on Hollywood, the Revolving Restaurant high above the Holiday Inn, in Hollywood. This hotel is currently known as Loews Hotel, in Hollywood. From the Windows on Hollywood Restaurant stage, it was plain to see Grauman's Chinese Theater, Hotel Roosevelt, and the Hollywood Bowl. Many Celebrities, Producers, and the Hollywood Crowd would stop in. Meeting many movers and shakers from back in the day, was very exciting!

This is where my career was coming full circle. I contacted my former Director from "A Little Night Music", Mr. John Bowab. Mr. Bowab recommended me to the Vincent Chase Actors Workshop. While at the Workshop, I began auditioning for parts in films. I released an Extended Play Dance Record. There were a few agents interested in representing me for films and commercials. Things were looking up…

Trump Castle Atlantic City, NJ | Sahara Resort, Las Vegas, NV

Indoor Marquee, Sahara | Cover Design: Las Vegas Image

Windows on Hollywood

Drama Logue Interview | Vinyl Extended Play

One afternoon, I received another call from Pat Merl to replace a Production Singer on a Carnival Cruise Lines ship that ported in Los Angeles. A replacement was needed as soon as possible. The contract was "temporary". However, this began my continual exclusive contracting with Carnival Cruise Lines, through Miller Reich Productions.

CCL Jubilee Headliner | CCL Jubilee Production Show with George Reich Dancers

"Midnight Special" CCL Celebration | "Midnight Special" CCL Celebration Orchestra

Aruba, "Champagne" Miller-Reich Productions | San Juan, PR "Champagne" Miller-Reich Productions

Also, during this "temporary" time period, Miller Reich Productions contracted me away from CCL, for one of their shows in Aruba. When that show closed, it was time to contract again in Puerto Rico, at the Sands Hotel and Casino. Next, back to CCL for an exclusive and extended period.

A highlight for me during this time period was to be recommended for U.S. Coast Guard Service and Seaworthy Training. Upon completion of the course work, I attained U.S. Coast Guard and International Waters Certification with installation as an official USCG Safety Survival Craft Crewman, under Liberian Registry. If we were to have mishaps at sea, my USCG Certification and Liberian Registration would be called upon to serve distressed passengers and crew.

I also found the time to become a Certified Diver, with my fellow dancers, while we were performing two shows a night at the Concorde Hotel, in Aruba.

Another fun adventure was to take flight lessons while in the Port of St. Thomas, aboard the CCL ship, MS Celebration. Was ready for my Solo Flight, when transferred back to Port of Los Angeles.

After much singing, sailing and going through the Panama Canal three times, it became apparent to me to depart from the Ports of Call, and the Luxury Cruise Liner lifestyle. When I finally disembarked from CCL, in the Port of Los Angeles, it was time to "hang up my tap shoes" and try something new. I then moved back to the Twin Cities to be near my family. Being near family and old friends on a daily basis helped me to give myself a fresh start. At this point, I decided to apply my talents to a career in broadcasting.

CHAPTER 4   PART 3

BROADCASTING AND BEYOND

IT WAS THE Fall of 1993. I enrolled at Brown Institute School of Broadcasting in Minneapolis, Minnesota. I Graduated with Magna Cum Laude Honors in the Summer of 1994. My first Radio job was at KDMA-KMGM-KKRC in Montevideo, Minnesota. My formal titles were News Director, On Air Talent and Reporter. Working at the radio station was the new lease on life that I had longed for. Then, by chance, I met someone.

Brad Fader had just returned to the city of Montevideo from Albuquerque, New Mexico. He returned to run the Monte Motel. This was his family's business. Our commonality was that we had both recently returned to the state of Minnesota after having lived out west. We were both, deep in our hearts, Minnesotans. I continued to work in radio, while singing at churches and at wedding receptions with a well-known Twin Cities band, "Loose Change". Brad continued to run the family motel business.

A couple of years into our relationship, we survived the 100 Year Flood that plagued the Upper Midwest, in the spring of 1997. I almost died in the Flood of '97, from black mold infection. We almost lost the motel business during the Flood of '97, too! The Monte Motel property butted right up to the Minnesota River. As we were flooded out of the business, we wondered how we could ever bounce back from destruction. However, we did make a financial comeback. FEMA rented several rooms in the motel, in order to serve the entire community, ravaged by the disaster.

My husband and I married that same year in August. Soon after, we moved to Savage, Minnesota where we started new jobs. I worked at the Chapel of Love, located at Mall of America. Brad supervised Document Destruction, a shredding business. One of the Wedding Officiants for Chapel of Love was Pastor Paul Marzahn. Pastor Paul was looking for a part-time Worship Director for Crossroads United Methodist Church in Lakeville. Pastor Paul Marzahn and his wife, Deb, along with the congregation, decided to hire me for the job. I was awestruck!! To sing and worship God, and be able to collect a paycheck for doing so? This was beyond my wildest imagination.

One Sunday, I had a very unusual visitor at our church. We were always receiving guests from other cultures, such as Ministers from Africa, Haiti and more. However, at this service, we had a Jewish Rabbi visit. As was my job, with other church leaders to greet incoming guests, I made eye contact with The Rabbi. The Rabbi ignored the other greeters in front of me and walked directly to me. I shook his hand, welcomed him, and escorted him to a vacant seat. He paid attention to the service, and our music leader asked me behind the altar, do you know the Rabbi? He is watching your every move! I shook my shoulders as if to say, "I don't know". After the service, the Rabbi waited for me, so that he could say goodbye. I went to ask him if he would like to meet with Pastor Paul. He shook his head, as if to say, "No". I asked again. This time, his eyes became steel grey and harsh. He said in a loud, gravelly voice, "No!" I deflected carefully, saying, "Ok, Ok, no problem, that's just fine. There is no reason to meet our pastor. Thank you for coming to the service." I walked him to the exit and watched him leave in a very nondescript compact car. Before he entered the car, he turned, and waved goodbye to me. I waved back.

As I walked away, the hairs on my neck were standing up. I had been through this type of interaction with the eyes of the Rabbi before! I realized that the Rabbi had been Mr. Frank Rosenthal. I believe that he made the trip to see me, as I had recently sent him an email, thanking him for my previous employment at Stardust Hotel and Casino.. It was a pleasant email, detailing our positive interactions throughout my contract. Nothing about the difficult times. In the email, I told him about my work history, culminating in my employment as Worship Director for Crossroads United Methodist Church. Soon after the visit, other co-workers who still lived in Las Vegas told me that Mr. Rosenthal liked to travel to Las Vegas casinos dressed as a Rabbi, so he could enjoy himself undetected. I feel peace in knowing that he did make the visit. I will go to my grave knowing he stopped by…

The words of Jesus:

> *Look, I am sending you out as a sheep among wolves.*
> *So be as shrewd as snakes and harmless as doves.*
> *But beware…*
> *This will be your opportunity to tell the rulers*
> *and other unbelievers about me.*
> *For it is not you who will be speaking-*
> *it will be the Spirit of your Father speaking through you.*
> (Matthew 10:16, 10:20)

Some years later, I started my own wedding shop. It was a beautiful shop, but a financial failure. Needing to get back on my feet financially, I then took jobs at the local Burnsville Mall. All the while, I continued to sing as a soloist for sporting events, political events, Veterans Events and at several churches. Again, things were looking up…

Ask Yourself…

- *Am I willing to sacrificially practice developing my passion?*
- *What am I passionately interested in?*
- *Am I determined to grasp firmly to my identity as a child of God?*
- *When I am tempted to be immoral, unethical, or selfish, will I reach out to another virtuous person for wisdom and accountability?*

Brad and Debra Lee-1997, St Joseph's Church, Montevideo, MN

15 Year Anniversary-2012 UMC Church, Montevideo, MN

Our Story-Sportsmen Inn | Brad Fishing 2022

Pastor Paul Marzahn and me | Outreach Worship Band, "SERVANT"

Event Band, "Loose Change" | Liturgical Duo, Barb Morseth and me

Metropolitan Stadium ...

Twin Cities Metropolitan Stadium

National Anthem MN Twins Game

Reciting the Pledge of Allegiance at MN State Capitol, on Capitol Steps, in St. Paul, MN

Former Speaker of the House, MN State Representative, Steve Sviggum and me on Capitol Steps

At the Podium-on Capitol Steps, Singing National Anthem for Live Event

With Jason Lewis, reviewing program notes for a Live Event

Singing National Anthem for Races at Canterbury Park Race Track with Dedications to Gold Star Families

Worship Cantor and Service Leader for Veterans Sunday Service during "The Traveling Wall" Event-MACV

Providing Patriotic Entertainment at Fort Snelling Military Basecamp, with Director for MACV Kathy Vitalis

Conversation with Larry Tillemans- Designated Military Clerk Typist for the WWII Nuremberg and Dauchau War Crimes Trials

WHEN EVERYTHING FALLS (LITERALLY), YOU NEED GRIT!

RIGHT BEFORE CHRISTMAS in 2006, the fall came! I had been having some problems earlier in the summertime with my foot falling asleep, but then I would just shake it off, go to work, go swimming and do my daily things. I was walking like there was no problem.

Shortly before Christmas, I went to get out of bed and I fell to my knees, and then I fell on my face. I couldn't move anything. My hands were near the sides of my face. I was face planted on the ground. From the elbows down, I was able to move my wrists, hands and fingers. I had to pull myself with my fingernails and my hands to the nearest phone. The rest of my body was a dead weight. I was laying on my belly pulling myself forward. I finally got to the phone.

First, I called Brad and I said, "I can't move. I am on the floor. Something is desperately wrong."

He said, "I'll be there as soon as I can be. You better call work so they're not waiting for you."

I called work and I told my manager, "I can't move. I can't walk. I'm lying on the floor."

He said, "Oh, you are? Well then, just crawl in here and tell me all about it."

I said, "No, I'm serious. I can't move."

I was taken to the emergency room, but they couldn't do anything for me. They didn't know what to do.

After a whole hour of being completely paralyzed, suddenly, it went away, and I was able to stand up. I was able to walk. This pattern went on throughout the holidays. I'd be fine, then, suddenly it would feel as though my spine was a zipper, being unzipped. I'd fall to the floor, or to a chair, if one was near. Then, I'd wait out the paralysis, and try to continue whatever I was doing. Soon, the times of paralysis were becoming faster and would last longer. It was as though I was experiencing labor, before birth. Unfortunately, there was no birth. Only complete paralysis. Of course, my husband and I tried to seek medical help, but were given no concrete answers.

I tried to go back to work, and then suddenly, I would have to lay down on the floor. My co-workers would call for security to put me in a wheelchair, so I could be wheeled to the nearest store entrance. My husband would have to leave his job and take me to the hospital. At the hospital, there were no answers. Such of a long wait, in the emergency waiting room.. No assistance whatsoever. We would give up waiting, and just go home. Always hoping for better luck, tomorrow.

Right before Christmas Eve, I was in the parking lot trying to walk into work. It was snowing. I felt my spine "unzip", and down I went. There was no choice but to lay on top of a snowbank. Finally, a good Samaritan contacted store security. They brought out a wheelchair, and somehow, sat me in it. We waited for my husband to once again, take me to the hospital. It was just unbelievable.

At the hospital, my husband, Brad, found a wheelchair, and wheeled me into Emergency. It was extremely crowded. We resolved to wait it out and sat for hours. Admissions was not calling my name. Once again, out of exhaustion, we went home.

Later, we found out that the hospital ER was refusing to see me, because of my changing insurance policies. The only physician who would help me without insurance, was my Internal Medicine physician, Dr. Gary Brunkow. He was testing me, and we were paying for tests out of pocket. On January 1st, 2007, when my Insurance renewed, the policy started to pay my bills.

By January, after several visits to Dr. Brunkow, my organs were starting to shut down. All I could do was sleep and try to make it to the Clinic for more tests. The situation was very dire. We had ruled out several auto-immune diseases, among them, Multiple Sclerosis. I had an MRI. The findings were visible as a neurological breakdown, but still no clear answers. Finally, I was tested for Lyme. One of the blots came back positive for Lyme.

Dr. Brunkow immediately gave me a shot to combat the venom in my system. Whatever was in the shot did help me to feel a little better. We set up two more appointments for the shots. The shots were very painful, but my organs were responding to the treatment from the daily shots. My Doctor then ordered a two-month round of infusions of the medicine and steroids needed to knock out the Lyme venom. I began to feel better and slowly got back on my feet. After two months, I slowly started working again.

During this health scare, we decided that our lifestyle and pace of living in the Twin Cities, was too difficult to maintain. We needed to have a less pressured and restorative pace for everyday life. We decided that rural living would be more suited to our needs. We made plans to buy back the family lodging business. We sold our house in Savage, MN and relocated back to Montevideo.

We took over the business, now called the Sportsmen Inn. I regained my ability to walk toward the end of 2007. I walked for six months with minimal problems, but then started to reverse back downhill. Should I have had more steroids? Another round of infusions to try and wipe out the weakened autoimmune condition again? Medical physicians had zero answers as to what to do. There were no prescriptions available to help me.

As the months progressed, I just got worse. I saw the top neurologists in our state. My MRIs would always show the same pattern of neurological distress. However, not a clue to indicate a bonafide neurological disease. All appointments were inconclusive. The one thing that every specialist agreed upon, was that my internal medicine physician, Dr. Gary Brunkow, had saved my life.

Within a couple of years, I was referred to a neurology specialist in Central Minnesota. After several extensive tests, a spinal puncture was given. The specialist misread the results from this test. The markers in the spinal fluid contain neurological markers for disease. If you have 6 bands or more of what is referred to as a cloudy fluid, you have MS, but he misread the chart. Unfortunately, I had 13 bands of cloudy fluid. However, due to the misreading of the indicators, once again, I was left to deal with inconclusive results.

The mistaken doctor told my husband, " She doesn't have Lyme in her bloodstream. She has normal spinal fluids. She just wants your attention. She is just being difficult and is making this up. There's nothing wrong with her. She is perfectly fine. Just ignore her." This was a prime example of medical gaslighting!

Believing what the specialist told him, Brad would try to encourage me to walk around a circular country road with him. The distance was one mile. At the halfway mark, there was a fire hydrant. I always had to stop and sit down on the fire hydrant.

Brad would say, "What are you doing? Come on. Try a little harder. The doctor said you're making it up." I said, "I can't go anywhere. My body will not move."

I'd then try to walk with jerky movements, and he'd say, "I know you can try harder. You are making this up, again." Then, he'd briskly walk home, get his truck, and come back to where I was waiting for him. He'd help me get into the truck and drive me home. I was prescribed walking sticks. I kept doctoring and searching for answers, but I wasn't getting any better.

Finally, just by chance, Gregg Waylander, APRN, CNP at Montevideo Clinic, took a look at my chart when I was having a very bad cold. He had recently lost his wife. She died from a brain tumor that was originally misdiagnosed. He conjectured that I might be misdiagnosed. "I am treating you for your bronchial condition, but I am also making a recommendation for you to be seen at the Mayo Clinic. Gather all your test results if you have copies and arrange them into a three-ring binder. There is something neurologically wrong with you. The specialists you have already seen haven't been able to uncover it. The only doctors that will figure this out are at Mayo."

I went to the Mayo Clinic in Rochester for a two-week period, and they did all sorts of tests. However, the researcher that was researching results from the past tests notebook that I brought along with me to Mayo, saw that I had 13 bands from my spinal puncture, that had already tested cloudy. She said, "I don't need to put you through the spinal puncture test, again". I was very grateful, as that test is not an easy one to take.

Mayo physicians put me through several neurological and blood tests. Also, three MRIs, and CT Scans. Two weeks later, the conclusive results were verbally handed down, "You have multiple sclerosis."

Specialists then fitted me for some braces on my back, my feet and my legs. At least I had a diagnosis at that point. I was so grateful to know the truth. I could relax knowing that MS was the answer.

ONCE I KNEW THE PROBLEM, I HAD TO CHANGE MY LIFESTYLE

AS I SAID in previous chapters, I had developed grit. I passionately wanted to overcome my MS limitations. This determination would require persistence, perseverance, patience, and practice. Courage was the most important ingredient. God would quietly remind me of this daily. Occupational and physical therapy would become constant practice for my brain, muscles, and in relearning simple tasks like walking, and taking care of my personal needs. I was determined to win this fight. Brad also had to work with me in achieving results. He also had to support me in our homemaking.

We had an occupational therapist come to our house with recommendations to remove furniture, in order to achieve a barrier free floorplan. I needed to use a walker throughout our homelife and make other changes. We were running a home-based business at that point. We lived in the management quarters of our Sportsmen Inn.

Occupational Therapists told my husband, "She can't be routinely taking care of the Front Desk at Sportsmen Inn after working full time at the Montevideo Chamber, all week. Adding to this, she's the Montevideo Mayor. We must give her some space at home, to relax. Any extra work activity must be put to a halt". Thankfully, it was...

Originally, when we moved back to Montevideo, in April of 2007, I started working at Walmart. I became manager of the Photo Department and Brad was running the Sportsmen Inn. When I would come home, I'd try to help clean, or tried to help out at the Front Desk. By the beginning of 2008, I started to decline in mobility, again.

Two years later, I was elected Mayor of Montevideo, and started to work full-time, once again, at KDMA-KMGM-KKRC. The regression in mobility was becoming noticeable, and permanent. I was seeing Specialists and the best answers they could give: "Use walking sticks and a cane during the daytime. Use a walker at night. Maybe a few walk aids can help you."

I then took a full-time administrative job at the Montevideo Chamber. A desk job. My diagnosis from Mayo came in the Fall of 2013. I had spent seven years without a proper diagnosis, and the disease had progressed. Without the constant prayer from others, and my faith filled attitude, I truly believe this disease would have ravaged my body completely. The Power of God would always intervene, as each physical step I tried to take became much more difficult.

I have discussed with my mentor in this book, Dr. Larry Kefauver, who is also a pastoral counselor, what it took to adapt and change. We put together the "10 Laws of Change" that are revealed through scriptural wisdom. Here they are...

1. *Change* means...to do something **new** you must let go of something old.

"Do not remember the former things,

Nor consider the things of old.

Behold, I will do a **new** thing, [I am changing things],

Now it shall spring forth;

Shall you not know [perceive] it?

I will even make a road in the wilderness
And rivers in the desert.
(Isaiah 43:18-19)

The word "new" also means "fresh or renewed" like fresh air, fresh baked, fresh water, etc. Our new life required us to let go of some of our old plans, dreams, expectations, and desires. To do that requires grit…a determination to not let the past determine our future. We were grateful for all that God had done in the past. It's worth remembering what God's will is for us, "Rejoice always, pray continually, give thanks in all circumstances for this is God's will for you in Christ Jesus."[5]

Don't camp out in the past!

Forget [don't obsess over; mull over and over again] the past…." "Stop dwelling in what's happened; plan, process, and proceed toward God's future."

Let go of the DUCKIE! *What?* You say. In Sesame Street, Hoots the Owl to Ernie: "You got to put down the duckie, If you want to play the Saxophone."

2. *Change* will cost you time, money, and relationships.

Change Counts the Cost. In Luke 14:28, Jesus instructs, "For which of you, intending to build a tower, does not sit down first and count the cost, whether he has enough to finish it." We had to change careers and restructure our entire financial budget.

3. *Change* requires new perspective, plans, process and people.

Our finite and limited perspective isn't enough to see long-term risks, benefits, outcomes and consequences. We need wise, godly counsel from others who understand how to apply God's truths to life situations. Isaiah 55:8-9, speaks about God's perspective, "For My thoughts are not your thoughts, Nor are your ways My ways," says the LORD. "For as the heavens are higher than the earth, So are My ways higher than your ways, And My thoughts than your thoughts."

4. *Change* demands focus.

Who or what is your focus? We read in Hebrews 12:1-2, "Therefore, since we are surrounded by such a great cloud of witnesses, let us throw off everything that hinders and the sin that so easily entangles, and let us run with perseverance the race marked out for us. **Let us fix our eyes on Jesus**, the author and perfecter of our faith, who for the joy set before him endured the cross, scorning its shame, and sat down at the right hand of the throne of God."(NIV)

The gritty person stays focused on the goal. My goal was to walk, lead an active and productive life in my work, family, church, and community. When I focused on Christ, I discovered His strength in my weakness, His provision in my lack, His wisdom in the midst of my confusion, and His peace whenever my days were in turmoil.

5. *Change* precipitates a fight!

Our earliest primal reflex in life is "Fight or Flight." Whenever I encountered health-related problems at home or work, I would often grow tired or blame others, or at times blame myself for circumstances out of my control. Perseverance means that we refuse to procrastinate, lose patience, or stop fighting. How do we fight? We start with prayer.

Eph 6:10-13

Finally, be strong in the Lord and in his mighty power. Put on the full armor of God so that you can take your stand against the devil's schemes. For our struggle is not against flesh and blood, but against the rulers, against the authorities, against the powers of this dark world and against the spiritual forces of evil in the heavenly realms. Therefore, put on the full armor of God, so that when the day of evil comes, you may be able to stand your ground, and after you have done everything, to stand.[6]

6. ***Change*** requires follow-through and finishing the job!

Here's what I have discovered in fighting MS which caused so much change in our lives.

- Go where you have never been.
- Do what you've never done.
- Risk more than you have risked-To achieve the impossible and to prosper beyond your wildest imaginations.

Focus, Fight, Finish!

In 2 Timothy 4:7-8, we read Paul's prescription of grit, "I have fought the good fight, I have finished the race, I have kept the faith." Often, we look at the word *fight* and think of different adjectives other than "good." However, remember that when God is with you in a fight, His plans for the outcome are *good not evil.* As hard, draining, discouraging, and tough your fight is, you will persevere when you know and declare, "The Lord is my strength and my strong tower."

7. ***Change*** involves others.

We need a team of supporters around us to impart to us strength, encouragement and wisdom. When going through change, reach out for help and get a commitment from others for help. Develop a support group of family, church members and friends not just colleagues or associates—people who agree with you, speak the truth in love to you, and will go with you!

CHANGE Requires the Right Friends

Psalm 1:1 reads,

Blessed is the man who does not walk in the counsel of the wicked or stand in the way of sinners or sit in the seat of mockers.

Remember that when significant change is required, some former friends may not choose to go with you. Don't try to persuade them; if they aren't with you in the change, they will hinder what God needs and wants to do in your life.

8. ***Change*** demands faith, hope and love.

The three irrepressible forces of change are faith, hope and love. Faith starts with trusting God completely. It's surrendering all you think you know for all that God eternally knows. You can trust His word and His Spirit to direct you toward making good decisions.

Hope puts your future into His hands as you obediently follow His ways. Hope knows that nothing is impossible when God is both the author and finisher of your faith.

Love ties you firmly to passionately love God, sincerely love others, and humbly love yourself. Because you place your confidence in the Lord, you must never throw your confidence away. Refuse self-doubt and blame. Renounce a spirit of fear because you have love, power, and a sound mind as you fight the good fight. Persevere. You are gritty.

1 Cor 13:13-14:1

3 And so **faith, hope, love** abide [**faith**--conviction and belief respecting man's relation to God and divine things; **hope**--joyful and confident expectation of eternal

salvation; **love**--true affection for God and man, growing out of God's love for and in us], these three; but the greatest of these is love. (AMP)

9. *Change* pushes us into God's Presence and ceaseless prayer.

CHANGE Is Becoming More Like Christ

Engrave this truth on your heart. Now the Lord is that Spirit: and where the Spirit of the Lord is, there is liberty. But we all, with open face beholding as in a glass the glory of the Lord, are **changed** into the same image from glory to glory, even as by the Spirit of the Lord. (2 Corinthians 3:17-18 KJV)

10. *Change* starts NOW!

"Watch for the Change, I am doing it Now!" (Isaiah 43:19)

Stop procrastinating.
Don't be afraid.
Refuse to be distracted.
Decide to trust and obey God.
Focus…Fight…Finish Strong

MOVING FORWARD WITH GOD

SO, OUR NEXT move forward, unchained from the past, was back to Montevideo and to repurchase our old family business which had changed hands twice. Monte Motel was now known as Sportsmen Inn. We became a well sought after lodging facility. A flourishing Family Run Business. We were always sold out. The Customer came first!!

In 2010, I was sworn in as Mayor of Montevideo. God worked out the impossible and used me to accomplish much. Most historic was my trip to Uruguay. The trip was arranged through the Montevideo, Uruguay Mayor, Ana Olivera, and Consul General of Uruguay, Dr. Nury Bauzan Benzano. This was a cultural exchange and was also hosted by Uruguayan Partners of the Americas and the U.S. State Department. Another trip highlight was meeting President of Uruguay, Jose (Pepe) Mujica, and his wonderful wife, First Lady Lucia Topolansky.

When I was originally elected Mayor, my prayer group initiated a yearly event that we held at City Hall, for the National Day of Prayer. During my final term, I had the distinguished honor to serve as Vice President for the League of MN Cities-Minnesota Mayors Association.

Being Mayor gave me the confidence to start the 501-c3 Charity now known as Diversity-USA. I direct theatrical shows that feature acceptance for different cultures within the community. We give to the local food shelves and other community needs. We strive to help the underserved and to bridge the differences between people and social groups. We advocate for Diversity, Equity, Inclusion, Accessibility and Disability.

Another new project is "Queen of Kindness"- my personal Blog website to launch my Book, Podcast and the Kindness Alliance.

In 2019, My husband and I retired to Lake Minnewaska, in Glenwood, MN. We have two grandchildren, a son and daughter-in-law. Heaven is a little closer in a home by the water. God has truly blessed us. Prayers of gratitude are offered every day!

Also, upon retirement, in 2019, I had the privilege of traveling to Paris, France for a marvelous Reunion at Lido de Paris. Seeing old cast members and meeting new ones, was just amazing, to say the least! The Reunion renewed my spirit to create a "Showgirl Makeover and Women's Empowerment Retreat".

Learning to walk again is my greatest personal accomplishment to date. Beginning in 2013, many therapists from CCM Health in Montevideo, Minnesota helped me to reach accommodation with my disabilities. When we moved to Glenwood, I began medical treatment at Glacial Ridge Health.

During the past summers of 2020-2023, there have been great strides with the help of Glacial Ridge Hospital Therapists, in Glenwood, Minnesota. I now look forward to continued rehabilitation during the Summer and Fall of 2024.

Aside from my Nonprofit Charity work, my goal is to help others with disabilities, or with any real or imagined obstacles, to live their best life!

Ask Yourself…

- *What new things are God doing in your life? Are you resisting or surrendering to His ways?*
- *What distractions to your focus need to be eliminated from your vision?*
- *What do you need from God to best fight your good fight?*
- *When will you decide to rely on faith, hope, and love instead of your own experience and knowledge?*

Blessed is the man who walks not in the counsel of the ungodly.
(Psalm 1:1)

"When you are facing self-doubt or uncertainty about how to proceed, a powerful way the people around you can help boost your capacity and confidence is by showing you what's possible."[7]

CHAPTER 6

CHANGING YOUR SUPPORT TEAM

My co-workers, community and church support teams were wonderful. How great were they? It was decided to run a mayoral campaign in the fall of 2010, and we won. I was having mobility issues, but it wasn't apparent. It just didn't seem relative to the citizens of Montevideo, or to me, for that matter. The citizens voted for me. The position of Montevideo Mayor is a non-partizan position. This fit me perfectly! I appeared in the 2010 Montevideo Holiday Parade as Mayor-Elect. I was sworn into office on January 10, 2011.

I was buoyed up emotionally because I was elected mayor, of course, but continued to decline, physically. I knew I had a job to do as mayor. Although the position was part-time, I pursued it fully. Nothing was going to stand in the way of my enthusiasm to commit to my town. The apparent physical change and bodily pain was going to have to make room for my new responsibilities as mayor. Since there was no concrete diagnosis for my condition, my personal summation would have to do. I kept thinking, "Maybe this was all a sign of aging?"   In early 2011, there was also an opening to fill at the radio station. It was so great to resume work there, again! The job entailed advertising sales, copywriting for ads and programs. Before putting the ad on the air, my favorite task was to perform the voice-over. It was so wonderful to catch up with past advertisers and greet the new.

When you are in radio sales, a big part of your day is spent in transit, driving to various businesses. You conduct face to face meetings with your clients. You are listening to the business owners and to their staff. You are discovering the new ideas that can be featured within their monthly story. The monthly story is usually fine-tuned into a :30 second ad, and quickly placed on the air.

However, as the months went by, and it was nearing the end of 2012, my health had dramatically declined. I knew it would soon be time to leave my full-time job at KDMA-KMGM-KKRC. It was just too phys-ically demanding. However, continuing to perform voice-overs upon request of clients, would not be a problem.

Another activity continued, was the production of a monthly radio show for Montevideo, called "Mayor's Corner". The show would feature guests from all over our local counties of Chippewa, Lac Qui Parle, Big Stone, Swift and Yellow Medicine. The focus was to keep people informed about what news and social interest was happening throughout the area.

It was also during this time period that I had a minor auto accident. I received medical attention and was told to rest up, as the minor whiplash may be causing greater damage to my spine. Neurologically, my symp-toms were going from bad to worse. Could the accident be the cause of increasing decline in mobility? There were no answers. I just had to "grin and bear" it all.

Campaign Signage | Fiesta Days Parade

2012 Aquatennial Queen honored

Monday was proclaimed Amanda Bertrand Day in Montevideo by Mayor Debra Lee Fader (left) in honor of the 2011 Fiesta Queen, who was recently crowned the 2012 Minneapolis Aquatennial Queen of the Lakes. Appearing with Bertrand, seen holding a plaque presented to her by Fader in recognition of her achievement and for being an ambassador for Montevideo as well, is her escort, Brent LaSalle, the 2011 Captain of the Minneapolis Aquatennial. (Staff photo by Judy Sperling).

New Mayor, New Aquatennial Queen Both representing Montevideo, MN

FROM THE OFFICE OF
MAYOR DEBRA LEE FADER

Welcoming Visitors to our City

Another life-changing opportunity was also extended during the month of December, in 2012. I was invited to make a Diplomatic Trip to meet our Sister City Mayor, Ana Olivera, in Montevideo, Uruguay. This all-expense paid trip had never been offered to a Montevideo, MN mayor before! Could I turn this down?

An all-expense paid, ten-day excursion to South America, to visit our Sister City? What a way to salute the end of 2012!

After much consideration at City Hall, it was decided that I should go. All additional travel expenses were paid through a grant provided by Uruguayan Partners, a US State Department cultural exchange program. Any other miscellaneous funds were paid by our Montevideo Convention and Visitors Bureau. What I learned on this trip could fill a book, all by itself!

Honoring our sister city

Consul General of Uruguay, Dr. Nury Bauzan (left) and
Montevideo Mayor Debra Lee Fader lay a wreath at the station
of José Artigas Sunday morning. (Staff photo by John Cross.)

With Dr Nury Bauzan, former Uruguayan Consulate, stationed in Chicago, Il. We are
standing in Artigas Plaza, Montevideo, MN, for Wreath Laying Ceremony honoring
El Presidente, Jose'Artigas, father of Uruguay, S. America.

Sister City Mayors at Montevideo, Uruguay City Offices. An official Press Conference
between Mayors, Ana Olivera and Debra Lee Fader

91

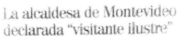

Montevideo, MN, USA Mayor declared "Illustrious Visitor" by
Montevideo, Uruguay, Mayor

Uruguayan President Jose'(Pepe) Mujica and First Lady Lucia Topolansky and me

News Clippings

News Clippings | Fiesta Days Intl. Wreath Ceremony with Uruguayan Dignitaries

When I left the radio station in early 2013, I really hoped to find a desk, or receptionist job. Fortunately, there was a temporary opening at Montevideo Area Chamber of Commerce. Taking on the position at the Chamber was a Godsend! Many of my organizational tasks could be accomplished by sitting at the Montevideo Chamber Reception Desk. There was definitely a learning curve, as it was my responsibility to create a monthly newsletter. This required a great deal of training in computer skills and graphics for me. I was so grateful for the new job. I took as much training available to learn the skills necessary to stay employed in the position.

While at the Chamber, my physical deterioration was definitely showing. People were wondering what was going on with me. I was on several boards throughout the community. I was very active in the political scene all over the state of Minnesota. Being unable to coordinate smoothly on my feet, was a true challenge. I could have given up, many times.

Regardless, I was lucky. People accepted my decline. I held a good front. My ability to serve our community was effective, as long as I could continue to sit down, while working at the Chamber. For public events, people accepted my use of a cane. Kindness poured, instead of criticism. I will be forever grateful to my community for accepting me, with or without proper mobility.

During the spring of 2013, I became very ill. I was having all sorts of bronchial problems. For many years, doctors treated my bronchial condition with a mixture of steroids and antibiotics. When given steroids, my walking seemed to improve. Not perfectly, but I could get up on my legs and walk, albeit with a cane, rather than having to sit down. Having another bronchial relapse during the summer of 2013, the repeated steroid treatment brought me to my "new normal" for wellness.

However, this time, things were going to be different. This time, I was armed with a medical referral to Mayo Clinic in Rochester. Maybe it was time for some answers. Maybe it was time to turn a corner. Maybe it was time to get off this treadmill of unanswered prayers. In my view, God was listening to petitions, and favoring a change. FNP Gregg Waylander made it possible for me to go to Mayo. I owe him a debt of thanks.

As stated earlier, I went to Mayo in September of 2013. There were two women doctors who diagnosed me with Multiple Sclerosis. There was a myriad of tests over a two-week time period in Rochester. My sister dutifully drove me back and forth to Mayo from St. Paul. Once fully diagnosed, my assignment was to find a reputable neurologist to treat my Multiple Sclerosis, within my area.

I immediately made an appointment to return to Dr. Noran. I had been seen by Dr. Noran a few years back, as he was recommended to me through my Chiropractor, Dr. Brad Moseng.

Unfortunately, Dr. Noran was booked. I chose to make an appointment with another neurologist. When I went to see the neurologist, he decided I didn't have MS because he didn't like the diagnosis from the two women doctors at Mayo Clinic. He had attended classes and graduated with both of the women doctors, from Mayo. He decided to disagree with their conclusions.

He said, " I'm not going to say that you have MS. I side with your previous neurologist. I agree with the doctor who told you, "it's all in your head."

His solution for me? "Come back to see me in three years. We can check then, to see if there are any other specific changes", he said. The doctor was also going to amend the Mayo diagnosis within my chart.

I was speechless! Thank God that my sister, Shelley, was with me. Shelley jumped into action, and pleaded, "Please don't do this. Debra Lee has been through hell. She has come to peace with this. She is resolute and relieved to know what is wrong with her. She wants to continue to make a living. However, if her MS becomes worse, at least she may be able to apply for disability compensation." Shelley continued, "If you make any changes to her medical chart, you will be keeping her in medical limbo. There will be no clear diagnosis."

My sister and I were shocked and truly angry. We finished the appointment, but not before making sure there were no changes placed into my medical chart. We were passionately committed to pursuing the in-depth and correct diagnosis from Mayo. We were determined to persevere. *No more medical gas-lighting allowed!!*

Not quite sure which way to turn for medical help, I embraced the quest to search for battery operated walk aids, and foot drop contraptions to keep me on my feet. Payment for the contraptions were all out-of-pocket, as they were considered experimental. I submitted to more X-rays, more MRIs, and more painful experimental testing. There were no medications available to me, according to each medical professional. I used canes at all times, and added a walker whenever required.

My ability to walk became exceedingly difficult. I was sporadically falling, tripping, breaking foot bones, front teeth, and tearing shoulder ligaments. My constant description of what it was like to suffer my condition, was akin to being the Tin Man from the Wizard of Oz. All my joints needed oil! I was becoming more rigid, and more injured, with each passing day. I took physical therapy for balance, and prayed not to trip, or to fall down.

During this time period, there were many political events centered around the sports of hunting and fishing. These events required a great deal of physical energy. Montevideo, MN is famous for outdoor sportsmanship. As mayor, it was my job to be on hand for all of the action. I did my level best to be a part of each event. I prayed myself through every activity. Spent days and nights coordinating VIP Hunts, singing the National Anthem at Warrior Boats Fishing Tournaments, writing a successful proposal for a second Governor's Pheasant Hunt, advocating for a full-service Veteran's Home in our city, and being voted onto the Executive Board for League of MN Cities-Minnesota Mayor's Association. Although my mind and energy to move forward for my City was unstoppable, my physical body was having trouble keeping up the pace. At times, I felt like "the little engine that could…"

Graphics: Derrick Schiff | With US Rep Collin Peterson MN Governor Mark Dayton

First Governor's Pheasant Hunt with Gov. Mark Dayton

By-Partisan Sportsmanship Clipping

With MN Governor Tim Walz | With US Representative Amy Klobuchar

With US Rep Tom Emmer | With US Rep Michele Fischbach

Finally, in 2016, I managed to get a referral to one of Mayo Clinic's satellite offices. I saw Dr. Kristine Kelly Williams. Dr. Williams took initial steps to prescribe oral prescriptions to lessen pain. Dr Williams also referred me to her practice at Edina Neurological Clinic in the Twin Cities. I was then introduced to Dr. Ylena Usmanova.

Dr. Usmanova was on the forefront of treatments for Multiple Sclerosis. Through her care, I found my specific diagnosis to be Primary Progressive Multiple Sclerosis. This means that my illness continues to progress every year. Dr Usmanova felt that I might be a candidate for a new drug, soon to be given FDA approval, upon completion of clinical trials. The drug, administered through IV infusions, is Ocrevus, made by Genentech.

I was part of the first group of patients in Minnesota to receive this drug. The therapeutic medication is administered every six months. This therapeutic has been a significant help to me. My first infusion was during the Summer of 2017.

My experience is that Ocrevus retards the progression of MS. Although I may not have the ability to walk normally, I am stalled from a rapid decline. My Primary Progressive symptoms have lessened.

Receiving the medication may take up to an eleven-hour process. What you do is receive Ocrevus as an intravenous medication at a hospital, and then go home to recover. The medication is a therapeutic monoclonal antibody infusion that fights your progression. A new scientific approach to treating MS.

At home, the first couple days afterward can be difficult. A patient can have reactions, but most are minor. MS affects the neurological system, through creating an overactive immune system. The medication really helps me to function, by taming this overactive auto-immune response. Ocrevus targets and tames a type of immune cell called a CD20-positive B cell, which plays a key role in the progression of the disease.

MS causes lesions to develop within your spinal cord and brain. MS creates an irritation that breaks down the myelin sheath that covers nerves. Sclerosis is an irritation that is going around in a circle. When I envision MS, I think about an oyster creating a pearl. When the oyster is irritated, it moves around to avoid the irritant, eventually making a beautiful pearl. Unfortunately, this activity within the human nervous system, does not create a thing of beauty. Instead, it creates a lesion.

The lesion is the product of the overly active irritant to the nervous system. Sclerosis creates the abnormal destruction of nerve tissue. Sclerosis, or multiple sclerosis is trying to remove any irritation and instead attacks the sheath that protects the nerves. Overactive sclerosis is trying to overly compensate to keep you well. This over activity causes your myelin sheath to break down. Sclerosis becomes more active and symptomatic when you are stressed, or tired.

As science has shown, you may not have enough Vitamin D in your system. Science is finding out new things all the time as to why people are subjected to MS. Another statistic that has been proven demographically, is that people who live in colder climates tend to be more susceptible to an MS diagnosis, as there is a lack of annual sunshine. It is not uncommon to be prescribed over 2000 units of Vitamin D, daily, as a boost to immunity. Another illness that is currently being linked to MS is Mononucleosis. There will be future discoveries.

Dr. Usmanova, and my current MS physician, Dr. Kathleen Rieke, both believe, as I do believe, that prayer has kept me from more harm than hurt. When it comes to my motor function abilities, God is in control!

I thank everyone who may have said a prayer for me throughout the years. You are my champions!!

Because of the power of prayer and the science behind my Ocrevus Treatment, I am functioning. Always determined to persevere, I also combine physical therapy to better my balance and improve my use of available motor skills. Ocrevus has retarded the growth of my lesions. Since 2017, my treatment has made me stronger and made it easier for me to move my body. Also, through Walk Therapy, I continue to try to correct my foot drop and manage my health in a much more practical way.

There have been many people on my support team to help me with my various choices for medical insurance, lifestyle changes, and motivating me to persevere with my treatment. *I am so grateful for each and every person who helps.*

I left my duties at the Montevideo Chamber of Commerce in 2015. I then took a part-time job as Office Manager for Entrepreneur Assistance Network and learned how to manage a nonprofit business. It was at that time, I decided to start my own nonprofit, Diversity-USA. We endeavor to bring positive attention to various Cultural Heritages, and the importance of respecting others.

We are a band of theatrical performers, musicians, and visual art creators. We encourage our audiences to **Celebrate Our Differences through Love, Hope, and Kindness.** We champion the underserved.

We give back with fund raising donations, goods, and services, to help our communities. Much of our charity work comes from our performances and multi-cultural events.

Diversity-USA, 501-(c) (3) Charity

Hollywood Music Box Show Ruth Ann Lee and me Photo: Mark Bauler

"Showgirl for a Day Retreat" With Sandy Lynn Erickson (L) and Jammie Niemeyer (R)Photo: VST Images-Victoria Tweeter

Hosting Membership Drive Pioneer Public Television PBS-Granite Falls, MN

Regarding my health condition, it is such a joy to get out of bed in the morning with limited pain. Thank you, Prayer Warriors and Ocrevus!

In 2018, my husband and I sold our lodging business. I finished my mayorship in 2018. After we sold our business, we moved to our renovated lake home and retired. During our retirement, we both keep active with our varied interests. Our biggest interest is in our family, and our grandkids!

My husband continues to hunt and fish. I continue with my non-profit work, book writing, and networking with other writers and artists.

I have been taking Ocrevus twice a year and continue with my Walk Therapy. My over-all life goal is to focus on being positive and inspire others to be positive, too.

Changing My Life and Lifestyle

As I have said, it takes grit to move from passion to perseverance as you grow and change in the midst of pain, rejection, and struggle. In my final chapter, we will walk through the process of change. How grit plays a major part as you transform yourself from tragedy into triumph.

Also, I will encourage you to understand how important prayer is, for your health and well-being. Prayer is a mystery. Prayer is also a manifestation of your thought process. Pray positive thoughts and pray in specifics, when you can. God does answer prayer. The more specific you are, the more God can do to help you.

Through my journey in refusing to be defeated with MS, my hope is that you can gain insight into how you too, can face life's toughest challenges. How you can become a victor instead of a victim!

Ask Yourself…

- *When I know that a change is needed, what makes me procrastinate?*
- *If people reject me and my motivations for change, how do I respond?*
- *Who are my key support people in helping me change and move forward?*
- *How does prayer strengthen and empower me in changing?*
- *Faith…who do I trust to walk with me in change?*
- *Hope…when I feel depressed and hopeless, what do I do?*
- *Love…how do I express my love for God, others, and myself?*

The Lord directs the steps of the godly.
He delights in every detail of their lives.
Though they stumble, they will never fall,
for the Lord holds them by the hand.
(Psalm 37:23-25 NLT)

The greatest accomplishment is not in never falling, but in rising again
after you fall.
-Vince Lombardi[8]

CHAPTER 7

PERSEVERE!

I DISCOVERED IN this rocky, tough journey the important necessity of perseverance. One way that Angela Duckworth explains perseverance is with the phrase "deliberate practice." That's what I do every day. I get up. I walk within my ability to do so. Then, practice my Walk Therapy exercises. I do all my daily tasks of self-care and homemaking, writing and sometimes even talking with *deliberate practice* despite pain or difficulty. Oddly enough, singing is still effortless for me.

> "My guess is that deliberate practice can be deeply gratifying, but in a different way than flow".

In other words, there are *different kinds* of positive experience: the thrill of getting better is one, and the ecstasy of performing at your best is another....

Each of the basic requirements of deliberate practice eventually becomes habit:

- A clearly defined stretch goal
- Full concentration and effort
- Immediate and informative feedback
- Repetition with reflection and refinement[9]

Practice is required on every level—body, soul, and spirit. Daily, I must practice most of the physical actions that many people take for granted. However, I have to work on my soul or psyche daily as well. I practice what Gary Chapman calls the *5 Love Languages:*

1. Words of Affirmation
2. Acts of Service
3. Gift Giving and Receiving
4. Quality Time
5. Physical Touch[10]

I must practice these love languages with others and with myself. My faith tells me to love others as myself. I remember a children's book entitled, *IALAC,* which stood for *I am Loveable and Capable.* If I don't care for and love myself, I will be unable to love and care for others.

Perseverance Begets Resilience

> *Not only so, but we also rejoice in our sufferings,*
> *because we know that suffering produces perseverance;*
> *perseverance, character; and character, hope.*
> *And hope does not disappoint us,*
> *because God has poured out his love into our hearts by the Holy Spirit,*
> *whom he has given us.*
> (Romans 5:3-5 NIV)

Perseverance is "stick to it" determination. It is a body, soul, and spirit dynamic. Spiritually, I discovered that I must be continually persevering in prayer. Paul calls it *praying continually.*[11] I would have so many people praying for me; we had all sorts of prayer chains at my church. I just was not going to accept, and roll over, and play dead. Defeat is not a component within my character. It is the spiritual component of perseverance. Never accept anything less of yourself.

I've just always felt with my life, and the struggles that I have been through, there is an order of learning within the chaos. I have pulled through and am here to help somebody else. God is leading my life. God will always see me through any adversity. I'm here for a purpose. Everybody has a purpose. We live. We learn. We pass on our personal experience and wisdom. God is helping me so that I can help others. As we learn, it is our duty to pass it on.

So, prayer is a critical key to persevering. Next, you must have a team around you... people around you who believed with you and who helped you. I discovered people encouraged me to persevere from my husband to people at church, to people that I was working with on the job and in the community. They elected me as Mayor; they believed in me. They saw the strength that I had and that I could still fulfill being the mayor despite my MS. They were with me rather than against me. They buoyed me up, made me stronger. Community can make a person stronger. Community helps you galvanize.

Whether it was physical therapy, whether it was getting out of the car, going to a meeting, there was always a push through the pain to do anything. To this day, I remember the slogan that my dance teacher had given me back in my junior high school years, which was, "Mind Over Matter." That's what she would say. If we were tired or if we were learning something new, and people wanted to just sit down, she'd say, "Mind over matter, people. Mind over matter." You had that expression in your head constantly. I've lived my life always referring to this phrase. Whenever times are tough, unleash mind over matter. Always, mind over the physical or psychological pain. You must learn to persevere.

What is matter? It is your physical body, mechanical physicality and your psychological limitations like frustration, disappointment, procrastination, and depression. My reaction to all of the tests, the tribulation, the pain, the suffering, all of the strife, is, "I'm not going to be defeated or controlled by my circumstances. With God as my Compass, I'm going to take control." My persevering attitude daily had to be *No* defeat. No quitting. No falling down and staying down. Rise to try again. Rebound. Be Resilient.

One writer said to me, "Webster's Dictionary defines resilience as the ability to *"bounce back from a difficult situation."* However, in my experience, I have known it to mean much more than that. To me, resilience means:

> *"Exercising the courage to consistently move through fear in the face of TEMPORARY oppression, opposition, hardship or adversity."*[12]

Remind Yourself: **2 Corinthians 4:17-18, "And This, Too, Shall Pass"** In other words, ALL THINGS ARE TEMPORARY…You can persevere.

At times in my good fight against MS, I feel like David fighting Goliath. The giant of my disease threatens to defeat and destroy me. Nevertheless, I persevere and discover that the character of Christ is forming in me. Giving me strength in my weakness and hope in the darkest of hours.

I am not a victim.
I am a victor!

YOU HAVE A CALLING...A PURPOSE!

GRITTY FAITH IS rooted in passion and perseverance. Yes, my life has been filled with mountaintops and valleys, wins and losses, falling down and getting up. I have discovered that nothing is impossible with God's power, intertwined with the help and support of others who pray for you and believe in you.

Though you may be tempted to give up and quit, don't! You do have a calling in life for which you can be passionate. You are purpose-driven with a dream and unique set of plans from God which will cause you to prosper.

Many people just don't understand how to pray, when to pray, why to pray, what to pray, or who to pray to? Throughout the seasons of my life, prayer has been the one constant practice to help me get through the day, or night. I've heard people call me a "Jesus Freak", or a "Bible Thumping Goody Two Shoes". (I've also heard worse than that...). So be it!

Prayer is the only, and truly positive resource to turn to. Positive prayer has no nasty aftertaste. It is very doubtful that you will have to tread the "walk of shame", once you start the positive habit of praying for sincere spiritual guidance. It is not easy to remove yourself from slippery slopes, but in time, with the practice of prayer, you will coordinate your footing. Your double-minded thoughts will leave you. You will be guided along the path leading to your most fulfilling life.

Here are some personal observations I have made, along my own prayer journey:

- Be prayerful in all you think. *Prayer is the manifestation of thought.*
- Be prayerful in all you do. *Prayer is the manifestation of thought and deed.*
- Be grateful in all you ask. *Grateful Prayer of Petition brings your life mercy.*
- Be merciful in all you seek. *Seek the merciful Face of God and Forgive.*
- Be forgiving in what you find. *Forgive and find power to "Let Go and Let God."*
- Be understanding to all. *Understand and accept that God's will is best for all.*
- Be loving to all. *Love overcomes hate. Love is the Golden Ticket to God's Favor.*
- Be peaceful. *Peacefully pray, "Lord Make Me an Instrument of Thy Peace".*

Pray your own prayer. Talk to God as if He was your closest confidant. You can tell God anything. After all, God is your Highest Counselor, and your Highest Confidant. God will never betray you!

Remember to end with "Amen". The Hebrew definition of "Amen" is "Truth" and "Certainty". It is an expression of agreement. "So be it".

If you are a new Believer, or a Cynic, take Baby Steps to God. Crawl and Drag yourself to God. You may kick and scream all the way toward God, but once you are near God, you will never want to go back. You will definitely know and feel the difference within yourself. **So, give God a try. What have you got to lose?**

(In my own experience, when I have been doubtful, what have I found to lose? The only thing to lose is an existence of misery and regret).

When all else fails-say this prayer. This prayer is prayed all over the world. This prayer has no religion. This prayer is practical. This prayer helps millions of people.   This prayer will help soothe your mind, spirit and soul.

SERENITY PRAYER

God grant me the SERENITY
To accept the things I cannot change,
The COURAGE to change the things I can
and
The WISDOM to know the Difference
Amen

Thank you for reading my book. My personal prayer for you is to
Live Your Best Life
and
Walk By Faith with God as Your Compass

So Be It-Amen

Best Seller List — Amazon 2023

Best Selling Book 2023 *The Keys to Authenticity*

Amazon Best Seller *Rise Up* **with Lisa Nichols**

ABOUT THE AUTHOR

DEBRA LEE FADER is a Music and Theater Graduate of the United States International University in San Diego, CA. She appeared in Las Vegas as the Principal Singer of "Lido de Paris" at the Stardust Hotel and Casino. She has also been associated with Carnival Cruise Lines performing her acclaimed Cabaret Act. She has performed Principal Roles in many American Musicals that have toured the United States and Canada. While performing in the Caribbean, she became a regular Featured Guest Artist on "Luis Vigoreaux Presenta", a popular variety show on WAPA TV, in Puerto Rico. She was featured in Puerto Rican films and was known as "La Chica de Chardon" for Chardon Apparel. Her voice was also featured pitching for an assortment of products heard or seen on Caribbean radio and TV.

Debra Lee Fader is proud to be from Bloomington, Minnesota. Debra served eight consecutive years as Mayor of the City of Montevideo, Minnesota. As the Ceremonial Head of the City, Debra Lee focused on Good Will and Kindness for all citizens.

Known as the "Singing Mayor of Montevideo", Debra sang the Uruguayan Anthem to visiting Dignitaries from Uruguay. Because of her Musical presentation, Debra Lee was invited to visit Uruguay for eleven days, as Official Mayoral Envoy. Debra was Official Guest of then Montevideo, Uruguay Mayor, Ana Olivera. While on Official Tour,

Debra also met the Uruguayan President, Jose' Mujica and his wife, Lucia Topolansky.

Debra Lee also spent time at the US Embassy with former Ambassador to Uruguay, Julissa Reynoso. This unprecedented Mayoral Envoy focused on Cultural Exchange between the two Montevideo Sister Cities. The Montevideo Sister City Relationship is the oldest in the United States, having its beginning in 1904.

Additionally, Debra Lee led Southern and Central Minnesota as Elected Board Advisor to Upper Minnesota Valley Regional Development Commission. She held Executive Board positions with Montevideo Convention and Visitor's Bureau, Montevideo Fiesta Days, Veteran's Home Advocacy, Beyond the Yellow Ribbon and Chippewa County Historical Society. As Visionary for the Montevideo Public Arts Projects which began during her years as Mayor. Debra is thrilled to see beautiful works of Public Art being created and presented throughout the City of Montevideo.

Her years of public service included installation as Vice President of the Minnesota Mayors Association. During this time, Debra Lee founded Diversity-USA, a 501-c3 Charity, honoring Social Diversity, Equity, Inclusion, Accessibility and Disability. This organization advocates for Cultural Preservation and Appreciation in Rural Areas. During the Covid-19 Pandemic, Debra Lee took to studies, and is now a Certified and Ordained Chaplain (IFIC-Cert/ABG Ministries, ORD-c).

A seasoned stage performer, director, radio and television broadcasting professional, you can catch her current performances at the Hollywood on Main stage in Montevideo. You can see and hear her interviews on many international Podcasts, including her own, "Recipe for Kindness". Or listen and watch her as a Guest Host during Membership Drives for Minnesota PBS Stations.

Debra Lee is married to Brad Fader. Both were proud to own Sportsmen Inn, a family owned and operated lodging business with a family-owned legacy of over 50 years. At retirement, the Inn was sold.

Now, Brad and Debra Lee welcome family and friends to visit their home on Lake Minnewaska in Glenwood, Minnesota.

With retirement, Debra Lee is busier than ever! Seeking a larger vision, she began Diversity-USA.Org. She can now advocate for Diversity, Equity, Inclusion, Accessibility and Disability within a much larger demographic.

Another start-up is ShowgirlUSA.Org. This Workshop and Retreat focuses on a Self-Care for women interested in Showgirl Glamour and Secrets.

With a new moniker coined from a dear friend, Debra Lee is ever grateful, and currently launching the "Queen of Kindness" Website, Blog and Kindness Alliance. Her personal memoir, "Walk by Faith" will be available on Amazon, Barnes and Noble, and Xulon Press.

How to Get Over It; Get Beyond It; Get It Right for Life

Table of Contents

MY EDITOR, DR. Larry Keefauver, a bestselling author, has an unpublished message that he has given permission for me to use to encourage and equip you with. I pray you will find these insights helpful as you live out "Mind Over Matter."

INTRODUCTION

You Can Get It Right!

I AM EXCITED for you. These stories will empower you to release your past, go beyond where you may be stuck in the present and move into a lifetime of making right decisions while eliminating bad choices and mistakes.

I'm not saying you will be perfect all the time. But know this. You have the power through the Holy Spirit and the wisdom, knowledge and understanding through His Word to make right decisions. Wouldn't you like to live like the psalmist?

> *Your word I have hidden in my heart,*
> *That I might not sin against You.*
> *Blessed are You, O LORD!*
> *Teach me Your statutes.*
> *With my lips I have declared*
> *All the judgments of Your mouth.*
> *I have rejoiced in the way of Your testimonies,*
> *As much as in all riches.*
> *I will meditate on Your precepts,*
> *And contemplate Your ways.*

I will delight myself in Your statutes;
I will not forget Your word.
Deal bountifully with Your servant,
That I may live and keep Your word.

(Psalm 119:11-17)

It is possible to know His Word and through the power of His indwelling Holy Spirit to obey His Way.

I invite you both to read these stories. Then share this message with a friend. You can begin a wonderful journey today of…

Getting over it…
       in order to…
              Get beyond it…
                     so that you can…
                            Get it right for the rest of your life!

CHAPTER 1

GET OVER IT

DON'T PUT YOUR mind on a shelf!

Just because you are passionately in love with Jesus and excited about living the Spirit-filled life, you don't have to stop thinking. Following Jesus involves both your heart and mind.

My wife, Judi and I met at an Ivy League school, the University of Pennsylvania, in a Bible study called InterVarsity Christian Fellowship. I discovered out of my mainline, "heady" upbringing and education that one could passionately love God and love His Word while not putting one's brain on the shelf.

We can think. Now thinking doesn't always get us where we need to go, but some Christians have so much heart that they have switched off their brains.

That's why some of us get involved in situations we shouldn't be in, and then as a counselor I ask, "What were you thinking?" You weren't - which is why you got in the situation.

God has given you a renewed mind so that you can be proactive and make decisions before you get into difficult situations. For example, if I were to lose everything tomorrow materially, I already know what I would do. I would give Him praise. I would honor Him. I would follow the next step because there is a reason for the lack. I know that whatever the enemy takes away and steals, he has got to restore seven times.

So enemy, don't dare touch what belongs to God's children because you have got to give it back.

Sometimes, You Will Hit the Wall

There will be seasons in your life when you hit the wall. I don't care if you have been baptized in Holy Spirit for years, if you know the deep mysteries of God's Word and you have been completely immersed and inundated in the anointing. I have counseled with pastors and leaders of large ministries all over the world that hit the wall, and when you hit the wall you have to know what to do. If you don't know what to do when you hit the wall, the enemy will attack you, oppress you and overcome you with things like anxiety, worry, depression, despair, hopelessness, anger and bitterness.

I thought that when we moved over from the mainline denomination and we were Spirit-filled, that Spirit-baptized believers would have less problems because they knew the Holy Spirit. I discovered that's not true. All of us have a soul, and that soul has strongholds in it. (Read 2 Corinthians 10.)

God is doing a work in you until the day you cross over into heaven. You are an unfinished work. Say to the impatient people in your life, "Please be patient with me. God isn't finished with me yet."

Psalm 18:28-29 declares, "For You will light my lamp. The Lord my God will enlighten my darkness. For by You I can run against a troop. By my God I can leap over a wall. As for God His way is perfect. The Word of the Lord is proven; He is a shield to all who trust in Him."

By God, I can leap over a wall. I don't have to hit the wall you can leap over a wall. However, you have to know before you get to the wall when to jump, or you will be flattened against the wall. Let me tell you what a wall is. A wall is a seemingly impossible situation which brings into your life hurt and pain that you don't believe you deserve. Even when you hit a wall that you know you are responsible for, it's hurtful and painful.

But that doesn't bother you nearly as much as the wall that you hit and you say, "God, I didn't deserve this."

"God, I have been tithing, but here's the wall."

"God, I have been living righteously, but here is the wall."

"God, I have been treating other people right, but I have just hit the wall."

"God, I have been living for You, but I have hit the wall."

I want to talk to you tonight as a pastoral counselor. When you hit the wall what do you do? Because you will hit a wall. There will come a moment in your life when you slam into a wall of hurt and pain that must be faced.

You will it walls as you follow Jesus. That's the truth. The truth isn't an easy thing to swallow. Living the Christian life isn't all dancing and praise and joy. All of us know that we are to respond to suffering and trials with joy and praise. However, some days we don't feel like praising and dancing and raising our hands. And…that's the truth!

So, once we hit the wall and before we can respond with joy and praise, what should we do? The first step, or the first act, or the first response is how to **GET OVER IT**. **IT** is always the wall. Whenever I say IT, it's the wall. IT is that thing that keeps you from stepping to the next thing.

IT is that thing that keeps you from getting into what God has for your tomorrow.

IT is that thing that destroys your future because you can't get out of your present. Are you understanding this? So the IT is the wall that sticks you where you are, and you can't move forward. You feel like your feet are in concrete, and you are sinking to the bottom of the Hudson River. You don't know what to do, and no matter how hard you swim, and no matter how deeply you gasp for air, it seems to you that there's no place to go. Ever been there?

So, when you hit the wall, I want you to know how to get over it.

Stop Dwelling in Your Past

First of all, let me tell you what the Word is. Here's what God says. Now, you may believe that this is not possible. I am going to show you the three ways it is possible so that you will never say that this is impossible again. The word is from Isaiah 43:19:

"Forget the former things. Do not dwell on the past."

Now, to forget in the Hebrew means "to forget!" It means to have amnesia. It means to "wipe the slate clean" and to never "bring past hurts and pain up again." The reason you live hitting the wall over and over again is because you can't get over. You are still remembering the past thing, the old thing. I don't care what it was.

For example, it may have been a moral failure. Do you know that every young person who loses his or her virginity because of immorality and fornication can start again and become pure by the blood of Jesus Christ? You don't have to live in the guilt and the shame of the past.

Do you know that just because you had a divorce it's not over? The unforgivable sin isn't divorce. The unforgivable sin is saying to the Holy Spirit, "You can't help me get over it." Such a statement blasphemes the person and power of the Holy Spirit.

Just because you went through a bankruptcy, just because you had a problem somewhere in a relationship, or because you were abused, abandoned or addicted, you can get over the past.

The reason you can get over it is because God by His Spirit gives you the power to forget it. Now, when you forget it, here's the decision you have to make. Tongue…speak to your tongue and say, "Tongue." You have got to speak to your tongue. Tongue, I refuse to speak that thing again. It's not denial. Denial is saying that it never happened. Forgetting is saying, "I forgot what happened." That's different.

The author, Keith Miller, tells the story of a Bishop in New Mexico who had a nun in one of his parishes where he was short a priest, and he had to put in nun in place of that. This was back in the sixties, and the Catholic Charismatic Renewal was exploding in New Mexico. She was a charismatic nun.

She was born of the Holy Spirit. Ablaze for God, she started ministering miracles, healings, deliverances and people being baptized in the Holy Spirit in her parish. And the Bishop was getting shown up by the nun because none of that stuff was happening in his diocese except in her parish. So, he called the sister in and sat her down. He said, "Sister, I understand that there are miracles, signs, wonders, healings and deliverances going on in your parish. How is that?"

And she said, "Well, I listen to the Lord, and I do what He tells me to do."

He said, "You hear from God?"

She said, "Yes."

"Okay. I want to verify this. Therefore, I am going to send you back to your parish, and the next time you and the Lord are talking, I want you to ask the Lord what the Bishop's secret sin is."

The only one who knew about this sin was the Bishop and the Lord.

"But if you are really talking to the Lord, then I can verify that He is speaking to you because that's the only way that you would ever know."

She said, "Yes, Bishop. I will ask Him when I go back."

So she went back, and the miracles, the signs and the wonders were increasing, and the power was flowing. But the Bishop didn't get a call from the nun. A month went by. Two months went by. Three months went by.

Finally, he couldn't take it any longer. He sent a message for the sister to come back to his office. She sat down there, and he said, "Sister, do you remember our last conversation?"

"Yes, Bishop. I do."

"Do you remember I asked you when you talked to the Lord? Have you been talking to the Lord lately?"

"Oh, yes. I talk to Him every day."

"Well, did you ask the Lord what the Bishop's secret sin was?"

"Oh, yes. I did exactly that, sir – just as you said."

"And what did the Lord say my secret sin was?"

She said, "Bishop, the Lord said He didn't remember!"

It's called grace. It's called forgiveness. He has put our sins away as far as the east is from the west. If He can forget, you can forget.

Forget the former things. Do not dwell on the past.

So, when that husband or that wife or that child brings up something that has been forgiven…when it's in the past, and they bring it up again, you say, "I am sorry. I just don't remember it. I'm sorry. I don't know how to talk about it anymore."

When the devil begins to accuse you and remind you of your past sin, you say, "I'm sorry. I just can't remember. I have forgotten it because the Lord has."

Decide to tell your tongue not to repeat what you have forgotten. Recall Isaiah 58:18-19.

"Do not dwell on the former things. See I am doing a new thing now it springs up."

Do you not believe it? That is the Word. What is your story?

It may be an adulterous life. It may be a failed marriage. It may be a disintegrating family. It may be a powerless life. In response to your circumstance, I simply have two words for you that you can use that are a psychological interdiction and interruption to your cycle of destruction: BUT GOD.

BUT GOD.

You don't understand, Larry. We lost everything.

BUT GOD.

You don't understand what a victim I have been in my life… how terrible my stuff has been.

BUT GOD.

It says in Acts 7:6:

"And the patriarchs being envious sold Joseph into Egypt…"

Ever gone down into Egypt? Ever hit the wall? The Word says:
…but God was with him.

That is the interruption to your cycle of self-condemnation so that you understand that it isn't you who has forgiven you. It's God who has forgiven you. And if God has forgiven you, it says in First John, "Beloved, if our heart does not condemn us, we have confidence toward God" (1 John 3:21).

> ***Why do you let your heart condemn you? For we have
> not been given this condemnation.***

Paul writes, "There is therefore now no condemnation for those who are in Christ Jesus" (Romans 8:1).

No condemnation.

Here is the response to this. When you get over something you have to do three things. Some of you are expecting a miracle without a response. You see God announces the miracle: "Take up your mat and walk." You have got to do something. You have got to take up the mat and walk.

Some of you are expecting for God to do what you are supposed to do. I have got to tell you something. God has already done for you what you need. The only reason you haven't gotten over it is because you haven't done what you need to do.

Aren't you glad you don't come to me for counseling? You thought that a counselor was someone who was just going to coddle you and comfort you and sympathize with you. I empathize with you, but you don't need my sympathy. What you need is my encouragement. And my encouragement to you is that you have got to take action. You have got to do something.

Respond to your past God's way. You can forget and not dwell in your past. There are three R's in response to your past. After tens of thousands of dollars of training, and clinical education, and looking at all the schools of psychotherapy, and being under supervision from everyone from psychologists, to psychiatrists, to a Jungian psychoanalyst, it comes down to just three things. This is not difficult to understand, but I want to tell you, it's hard to do. So, I want you to know that you are going to have to spend some effort to do this.

Step 1: Rejoice in What God Did in Your Past

> *Rejoice in the Lord always. Again, I will say, rejoice!*
> (Philippians 4:4)

The first response is to rejoice in what God has done. It says in Philippians 4 that we are to rejoice in the Lord some of the time? No, always. That means when your spouse is mean, rejoice in the Lord. That means when your teenager is a pain, rejoice in the Lord. That means when your boss does not recognize how much you are worth to the company, rejoice. That means when the pastor doesn't recognize the gift that you so proudly have and you wonder, "Where is the badge?" Oh, get over it, and just rejoice.

It may surprise you, but your church isn't the only place your gift is needed. Your neighbor needs your gift. Your colleague at work needs your gift. Your family needs your gift. Why don't you practice it there, so when it manifests there, it's really real?

Rejoice! Rejoice in what God has done. At the end of Genesis, Joseph says, "What the enemy intended for evil, God intended for good." That means in all things God is at work for good to them who love Him and are called according to His purpose.

I want you to know that when you are coming up to that wall, you shouldn't be looking at the wall. You should be looking for God. You should be seeing what God is doing because God has a way for you to jump over that wall. But if all you see is the wall, you are going to hit the wall.

When you hit the wall, it's because you are looking at the wall instead of looking at God Who is over the wall. In order to look at Him Who is over the wall, you must start rejoicing. For example...

> "Bless God. That opportunity for which I have no money is coming which means that God is going to prove Himself again. I rejoice in all things always."

The first step "to get over it" is to rejoice.

Step 2: Repent for What You've Done Wrong!

> *For godly sorrow produces repentance leading to salvation,*
> *not to be regretted;*
> *but the sorrow of the world produces death*
> (2 Corinthians 7:10)

The next step is when you look at the past and when you are dealing with the past you need to repent. You rejoice in what God has done, and you repent for what you have done wrong. It says in 2 Corinthians that godly sorrow brings repentance that leads to salvation.

Literally that means that repentance leads to healing. You see, every time you confess and repent as the Scripture promises in James 5, there is going to be healing that takes place. James 5:16 declares, "Confess your trespasses to one another, and pray for one another, that you may be healed."

You have tried to hide and cover up your sinful past. Don't hide it. Confess it. Speak it out. Only through repenting of past wrongs can lasting healing come.

You may protest, "Well, I don't want anyone at church to see this thing from my past."

I was counseling the wife of a deacon. Their marriage was falling apart. They had a picture perfect marriage. He loved her. She loved him. But for some reason they couldn't connect. Love wasn't enough.

It never is. There has got to be more. There has got to be a lot of things in marriage like trust and communication.

And she said to me that she was so ashamed.

And I am thinking, "Ashamed? You are a wonderful mother. You are the leaders in our youth group. You do things for the poor. You visit the sick. Your husband works and gives. You are kind." I mean, everything you could think of that a godly couple would be, they were. Yet, for some reason, there was a wall between them that they couldn't get over.

He came to me and he said, "Larry, I don't know what's wrong with my wife. There is something here. I don't know what it is. I must have done something."

So now I looked at her and asked, "Why are you filled with shame?"

And she said, "For years, my husband has bragged about me to others. He has told me how proud he was that we were pure before we got married, that we were both virgins when we got married. But I never told him. I didn't have the heart to tell him that before we ever met I had had an abortion. I know he would reject me if I told him."

So, I did the loving, pastoral, compassionate thing that any pastor would do. I picked up the phone, and I called her husband right then. I said, "Get in here. We have something to talk about."

And she looked at me and said, "I thought everything said in this office is confidential."

I said, "It is. I am not going to tell your husband anything. You are going to tell him everything yourself."

So, her husband came with her to my office. He was so excited that he was going to find out what it was that was keeping them apart in their marriage. He sat down, and he was just smiling. He was so confident that this was going to be a great thing. And in her tears, she told him what she dreaded for him to ever know.

And he looked at her, and he said, "I don't believe it!" And he started yelling at her. Now, this is my deacon. He was screaming at her and condemning her.

I stopped him, and I said, "I just want to ask you one question. I know Jesus died for you, but did He die for her, too? I know that Jesus has forgiven your wife. Can you?"

And about three hours later he repented of pride, which was the real wall in their marriage –not shame, which she thought it was.

It's called repentance. If there is something in your past that you've got to get over, just get it out. Confess it. Repent of it, because there is no shame in the cross. He bore all your shame. He was pierced for your transgressions. You're clean. Get over it. So, if you are guilty tonight it's because you want to be, not because you have to be.

Step 3: Release and Forgive

"For if you forgive men their trespasses,
your heavenly Father will also forgive you.
But if you do not forgive men their trespasses,
neither will your Father forgive your trespasses."
(Matthew 6:14-15)

"And be kind to one another, tenderhearted,
forgiving one another,
even as God in Christ forgave you."
(Ephesians 4:32)

First of all, we rejoice in what God has done. Then we repent for what we have done. Then we release whom we must forgive.

Release that person. That person doesn't owe you anything. His debt was paid on the cross of Jesus Christ. He has no offense now.

You may respond, "But he owes me an apology."

No. He doesn't.

"Well, he owes me restoration and restitution."

No, he doesn't.

You see, Jesus has already made the apology. Jesus has already made the restitution. Don't just say His name; use His name. When you call upon the name of Jesus, the past is canceled. You are commanded to forgive.

There are two things Jesus says are unforgivable: blasphemy of the Holy Spirit and unforgiveness. If you don't forgive those who have hurt you what does He say? "Your Father in heaven will not forgive you" (Read Matthew 6). I can't tell you how many churches we visit and those churches are filled with unforgiving, offended people. If you are one of them, you've got to get over it.

You may be offended with your pastor or you may be offended with the pastor of a church that you left. You have never forgiven him, and you just talk bad about him. But you need to know that you will never receive anything from a pastor in the church that you attend until you let go of your offense against an old pastor who hurt you.

Have offenses? Get over them. I don't care with whom you are offended. It could have been a father who raped you, or abused you, or abandoned you. Or it could have been a mother who criticized and condemned you. If you can't honor them, the favor of God is cut off in your life.

You are commanded to honor your parents if for no other reason than they gave you birth. You may not even know who they were, but I want to tell you something, if the only thing that comes out of your lips is, "I honor you, God, because You gave me birth through parents I don't even know," then let the rest that you feel, the rest that has happened be silent, because, in honor, favor is released and blessing. In dishonor, curse and destruction are released.

Before you can get beyond it—the wall that is blocking your future, you have got to get over it. You need to rejoice even when you don't feel like it. You need to see what God did in you and through the circumstance to really work on your life, to do a work in your life that could have never been accomplished without that. It's time to rejoice and thank God for all the good things in your past.

You may need to repent. You need to turn away from and let go of that sin, that guilt and that condemnation. It's time to release somebody you have been angry at, hurt because of, and it's time to get over it.

There is no easy way to do this. You just have to decide that now is the time to release or to repent or to rejoice. So, I am just going to do something real simple. If you fall into one of those categories, I just want you to stop right now. If you say, "I need to repent right now," or, "I need to forgive somebody I have been holding an offence against," just do it right NOW.

In doing so, you are admitting that you need to get over it. "I just need to get over this." It may be a father or a mother that you are still hurting and offended with after all these years. God wants to heal that wound in your heart. It's time to get over it.

"Lord, I repent. I rejoice in what You did. I release it, Lord." And if there is a person you need to release, don't let that person be the anchor that takes you to the bottom of the ocean of depression. Just let go of it right now. The Holy Spirit says, "It's over. It's over. You don't have to go back there any more. It's over. The hurt is over. Yes, it was real. But now it's over. You can get over it."

Now, just begin to thank Him. Just say, "I thank You, Lord. I thank You, Lord." That's called praise. I thank You, Lord. I praise you, Lord. I thank You for dying for me. I thank You for Your shed blood. I thank You that I can put my shame and my guilt at the cross of Jesus Christ. I thank You that I can forget the former things. I don't have to dwell there. You are going to do something new in my heart. You are releasing me in Jesus name. Amen."

Get over it. You can. You must. Do it now.

CHAPTER 2

GET BEYOND IT

Get over it…
in order to **get beyond it!**

IT'S TIME TO get beyond it. You just don't want to go over the wall. You want to get as far away from that wall as you can. There are three keys to get beyond where you are, because some of you are just on the other side of the wall. You've got your back against the wall. Every once in awhile you just look around and say, "Yep. It's there." You can't get beyond it because you still think about it every once in awhile. You still talk about it on occasion.

The only time that Judi and I talk about the pain of our marriage in the past is to use it as a teaching example to help others. We never go there. We are not just over the wall. We are beyond the wall. Are you ready to get beyond it? There are three simple keys to get beyond it. I am going to go concisely through these because I want you to get, not just beyond it, but I want you to get it right for the rest of your life.

Key 1: Live in the Now!

Here is the first key to getting beyond it. *Get beyond it by living in the now and not in the past… by redeeming the time* as we read in Ephesians.

> "*See then that you walk circumspectly, not as fools but as wise,* **<u>redeeming the time</u>**, *because the days are evil.*"(Eph. 5:15-16)

> "*Behold,* **now** *is the accepted time; behold,*
>   *now is the day of salvation.*"
> (2 Corinthians 6:2b)

Say, "Now." Some of you will not let go of it. You are living your past every day. You are saying the same thing your daddy said to you. You are saying the same thing your mama said to you. You are repeating the pain over and over again. Oh, you got over it, but every once in awhile you are not far enough beyond it, and you just sort of look back and check. You say, "Well, if you knew what I have been through."

God does not care as much about what happens to you as He does about how you respond to it. But here's what you do. "Oh, look at what's happened to me. These people are attacking me. My boss doesn't like me. My children don't appreciate me. I don't got no money. Oh, God…."

He says, "I don't care."

He really doesn't care, and the reason He doesn't care is because if He cared about your circumstance, He would be nullifying what He has already done. He already took care of your circumstance, and you are trying to get Him to focus on something that you think is real that's not real anymore.

You see, just because it's fact doesn't mean it's truth. Just because it's visible doesn't mean it's real. The things that are invisible are what's real in the kingdom of God (2 Corinthians 4), and if you are going to live in the now, you must see what God is doing right **now**.

For example, I must see what God is doing in my immediate conversation with my wife. Not what happened yesterday or years ago. God has forgiven. So have I. This means that in my *now* conversation, God must be at work as Lord and Savior or I will never go beyond now into God's future plans for our lives. If He isn't Lord over my *now*, He isn't Lord.

When God tells me to do something in the *now*, and I say, "No, Lord," it is an oxymoron. It is impossible to say, "No, Lord," because if you say "no," then He isn't *Lord*. The only appropriate response when He says to do something in the *now* is, "Yes, Lord."

Just practice it. Say, "Yes, Lord." When you say, "No, Lord," you have confessed that He is not your Lord at all. It is an impossible juxtaposition of words - NO LORD. The now is always, "Yes, Lord." He doesn't want a discussion. He doesn't want an argument. He doesn't want to try a court case with you arguing your side. He simply doesn't care about your circumstance.

You say, "Oh, Larry, that messes up my theology."

Then go back and read Job. Look at what all Job went through. And finally Job had had it, and he kept saying, "Now, God, why? Now, God, why?" Ever done that? Have you ever asked God why?

Don't ever question God again about your circumstances. Ask Him where He is going and what He is doing so that you might join Him. What changes where you are going isn't a change in your circumstances, it's a change in you.

When we question God about our now, we never get beyond it. God always handles those kinds of questions just like He did with Job. "Who are you to question Me? I created the universe. I put the foundations beneath the seas. I have done all of this, and you are asking me why?" Read it for yourself:

> "Then the LORD answered Job out of the whirlwind, and said:
> "Who is this who darkens counsel By words without knowledge?
> Now prepare yourself like a man; I will question you, and you
> shall answer Me.
> "Where were you when I laid the foundations of the earth? Tell
> Me, if you have understanding. Who determined its measure-
> ments? Surely you know! Or who stretched the line upon it? To

what were its foundations fastened? Or who laid its cornerstone,
When the morning stars sang together, and all the sons of God
shouted for joy?" (Job 38:1-7)

Stop wasting your time asking, "Oh, God, why?"

No! No, you ask God instead, "Where are You? I am ready to join you. I don't understand." And much of what God does is a mystery because, you understand, that what He is doing now is putting in order a series of events that have to be perfectly ordered for what's going to happen ten years from now.

You can't begin to completely understand the *now* because He is arranging the future so that when you get to the future, you will arrive in the right place. And there is no way you can understand the future, because you have got to go through the *now* to get to the future. Do you understand what I am saying? Just be obedient in the *now*.

"Oh, God, where is this leading?" you plead.

You don't need to know. For example, when Jesus told them He was going to the cross, they didn't believe Him. When He revealed the future to His disciples, they didn't trust Him. So, all He is saying to you is, "I want you to take that next step now in obedience."

And if the next step that God asks you to take is the opposite of the last step He asked you to take, go ahead and take it anyway. Very often the next thing that God asks you to do will be the exact opposite of the last thing He asked you to do. He said to Abraham, "Kill the boy." And just about the time he was going to kill the boy, God said, "Don't kill the boy." Can't you see Abraham thinking, "Will You figure this out? Would You just make up your mind?"

Here's another example. In Jonah 4, God gave Jonah a leafy plant for shade and the Bible says that the **next** day God allowed a worm to destroy the tree. The question isn't, "What's going to happen *next*?" The question is, "Are you going to be obedient when the *next* happens?" Ok? Live obediently in the now.

Key 2: Live for others not yourself.

"Through love," Galatians 5:13 says, "serve one another."

"Honor Christ by submitting to one another," Ephesians 5:21 commands.

Look at your neighbor, your spouse, child, pastor or boss and say, "How may I serve you?" You see, life is about serving somebody else. It's about living for somebody else.

Parents, you had children not to serve you, but to serve them. But then, when you serve them, and they don't appreciate it, you get angry. Why? You don't serve to get their approval, to get their praise or to get their gratitude. You serve them because they are the seed that God's going to use in the next generation. You serve them because they are all you've got to get there.

You are thinking, "I can't go home and say to my teenager, 'I am here to serve you.' He'll take advantage of me."

Do you know why you fear serving him? Because you raised him to be that way. If you don't like the way your teenager is now, look in the mirror, because you are the problem. If you don't like the way your teenager is just look in the mirror, because the teenager that you have is the harvest of what you have deposited in him or her from birth until now.

If you were depositing God, and only what God said, and only what God was doing… if you were depositing blessing, and never speaking curse… if you were always speaking life and never criticizing… if you were building them up instead of tearing them down… then don't you know that by the time they were fifteen, they would be building you up and not tearing you down because you get what you sow.

"You see, you don't understand, Larry. They got in with a bad set of company. They got in with the wrong crowd."

How do you think they got there? You let them get there. You put them in a place where they were in relationship with the wrong people.

The Bible never says teenagers have the right to choose their friends. Their friends are chosen by their parents.

"Honey, I don't want to interfere with the friends that you choose."

How can a thirteen year old have the wisdom, insight and intuition of a 35 year old, Spirit-filled parent? She doesn't know what friends she needs. How would she know? She hasn't lived thirty years or forty years. She doesn't see that the heart is deceitfully wicked and who can know it. You put that young lady with the Christian friends that she needs to be with instead of letting her choose anyone that stirs her hormones. Instead of letting your children go to their friends' houses, you have everybody in your house because there you can control the TV, and you control the radio, and you control the music.

You say, "Honey, if you want to go to So-and-So's house, I am just going to go with you the first time. I want to meet her parents. I want to sit in their living room I want to see what kind of videos they watch. I want to listen to what's in their CD's."

She says, "Oh, Mama, I don't want you to meet my friends. You would be ashamed of them."

"Then you can't hang with them, Honey."

Your children are not raising you. You are raising them. I know this isn't supposed to be a parenting seminar. This is just in me tonight. But some of you, you have got it all wrong. You want your teenager to be your friend. I want to tell you something. You have got to be his parent before he can be your friend. You are not here to please them. You are here to please God.

Don't ask your son, "Honey, how am I doing?"

Instead say, "God, how am I doing with Honey?"

Mama, you are serving them dinner, and they are serving you the dishes being cleaned after dinner. You are serving them electricity and water, so that they can serve you by putting the clothes in the washing machine and the dryer and putting them up.

Don't do for them what they can do for themselves because God never does for you what you can do for yourself. Some of you are creating dependency relationships with your children and with your spouse.

Hey guys, you didn't marry your mama. She's your wife. She ain't your mama. Pick up your own clothes, baby. My wife goes through the bedroom, and she looks at the pile of dirty clothes on the floor that I put there and she says, "Where's your mama? I don't see your mama anywhere here."

We serve others to teach them how to serve others.

Key 3: Live in faith, hope and love instead of doubt, despair and dependency.

This is so important. There are only three prescriptions for life… I don't want to call them drugs. I just don't know what else to call them… ointments. That sounds more biblical…ointments for your soul. There are only three balms that produce healing in your soul…only three.

I have been to some deliverance groups and all this mumbo jumbo, almost magical formulas are uttered with jumping up and down and foaming at the mouth. And possessed people will do weird things. But Jesus simply said, "Come out of him." He didn't have a lot of formulas. He had the same three things to work a miracle that you do. He had faith; He had hope; and He had love.

Every injured wound in your soul is going to be healed by one or more of these three things. Every doubt is healed by faith. Every untrusting relationship is touched by faith. Every moment of despair and depression and suicidal tendencies needs hope. And every rejected feeling needs love. Faith, hope and love.

When I am counseling with somebody, all I have to do is give a word of hope, and God enters the room, and the Spirit of God moves in that person's life.

I walked up to a man at the altar. I didn't know him. He was just weeping at the altar. And the Holy Spirit says, "Tell him, 'Daddy loves you.'"

So, I put my arms around him, and for ten minutes all I did was say, "Daddy loves you." And he was delivered from addiction, abuse and abandonment. He is serving the Lord today because he heard the truth, "Daddy loves you. Daddy loves you."

When you get beyond it by living in the now, when you get beyond it by serving others, you forget your selfish focus on your problems. I have noticed that when I start serving other people, I forget about my problems. Have you noticed that? I am so busy serving other people my problems just seem to go away because what I sow, I receive. What I minister, I receive in ministry. So, if I need mercy, I am given mercy. If I give money, I am given money.

I have to tell you this quick story. I was at an apostolic gathering. And when you are in these meetings, if you are called an apostle, you are supposed to act like one. Well, I am acting like an apostle. Glory to God. I didn't have my armor bearer with me because I couldn't afford his plane ticket, so I just brought my wife. Glory to God.

The week before that meeting I had been in the ER with chest pains because I was looking at my circumstances. I had less than $200 in the bank and nothing on the calendar for the year 2004. That can be disturbing. We are supposed to walk by faith not by sight. But sometimes, what we see can see or don't see can really upset us. We must remember that God is our source.

So, it looked like God had messed up. He had not seen my empty calendar. He did not realize that I didn't have any book projects sold. He didn't remember that I didn't have any speaking engagements. I mean, I had even placed a few calls with a few friends, and they said, "No, we can't use you next year." Now, that will get your ego, especially when you are an apostle. "No, we don't need you next year. Maybe the following year."

I began to worry. And I worried myself into the hospital. I had an Asian, a Chinese cardiologist from Hong Kong who was a Buddhist. Here I am, a mighty man of God on his back being taken care of by a Buddhist Chinese man. So, he ran all the tests on Saturday night.

Judi made me go in. I think she was doing that to me to confront me with the fact that physiologically I was just fine, but I had a spiritual problem. Nurses are like that. They don't mess with you, you know. If you hurt they say, "Get over it. Get up. I don't care how much it hurts." Nurses can be really mean when they want to be!

"Get out of that bed."

"I can't even walk."

"Get out of that bed. Start walking."

That's what Judi is like. She says, "You think you are having heart pains? Go to the hospital. I don't want you dying on my call. You die on their call."

So, the doctor comes in after the stress test and says, "I see here by your records that you are a preacher, a pastor."

I said, "That's right."

He says, "I have done all the tests, and there is nothing wrong. So, preacher, you tell me what's wrong with you."

Dr. Larry wasn't feeling like Dr. Larry right then.

So, I had been in the hospital, but nothing was really wrong with me physically. At this meeting I was one of the keynoters. I had to act like an apostle. I am broke, but I have got to act like an apostle. I have got to get up there and talk about investing in the kingdom of God and the glorious riches that are coming from heaven, and I am broke. I mean, this is a humbling situation.

At these conferences, they always find a way to take an offering. Have you noticed that? And it is not just an offering; it's a multitude of offerings. Well, bless God, five more dollars.

We are in the last meeting. I have keynoted. They are now doing a special love offering for the leaders to honor them. And I get out a check and Judi is sitting there praying in the Spirit with her eyes closed. So, she can't see what I am going to write on the check, and I am writing.

I am now down to about $145, and I am going to do something great. I am going to write a check for $100. Now, that's a big sacrificial offering.

Right? Doesn't that sound wonderful? Aren't you proud of me? And I write this check. I fold it over, and I am praying as if God is impressed.

And Judi looked up, opened her eyes, turned to me and said, "God just spoke to me."

And I thought, "Oh no! Oh, Jesus, no. Oh, God, no." And I said, "What did He say?"

"God said, 'You forgot a zero.'"

She had not seen the check. For all she knew I had written a ten dollar check and now it could be a hundred dollars. But when you go from $100 to $1000, now that's a big jump. Now, God may have been impressed with my gift, but I want to assure you that my bank would not be impressed with my gift the next week. When you give what you don't have, the bank doesn't just loan it to you. They bounce it around.

So I just tore it up. I put another zero in. I wrote it for $1000, and now I am praying in tongues. We are talking faith now. We are beyond expectancy. We are talking faith now. And they thought I was weeping out of love for them when I put that in there. But baby, I am weeping thinking, "Oh God, what am I going to do?" Has anybody ever done this thing? You know what I am talking about.

So, this is on a Friday. On Saturday, we are flying to a board meeting of University of the Family. We are on the board, and we are in this meeting, and the chairman of the board looks at me and he said, "Oh, Larry!"

Now, I am sitting there being depressed, and I am trying to have this fake smile. You know how you do. You come to church depressed, but you have this fake smile. And I had this fake smile on.

And he said, "Larry, I am so sorry. A couple of months ago I learned from the foundation to which we submitted your request to do a year-long study Bible that it was approved. They have approved a contract for you of $100,000. Here is the advance."

The reason the calendar was empty was because I had a study Bible to write.

God will get you beyond where you are at when your focus is on living obediently in the now, serving others and deciding to live in faith, hope and love instead of doubt, despair and dependency. Stop depending on yourself or others to show you the next step. Ask God. Seek His face. Hear His voice.

Jesus said, "Have **faith** in God." (Mark 11:22)
Only then can you risk trusting others.

Psalms 71:5 declares, "My **hope** is in you, O Lord God."
Only then can you stop expecting others to meet your needs.

"**Love** the Lord your God with all your heart, all your soul and all your strength" declares Deuteronomy 6:5.

Only then can you stop depending on others and begin truly loving them for who they are not for what they can do for you.

Get beyond it…so that you can get it right for the rest of your life!

CHAPTER 3

GET IT RIGHT FOR LIFE

NOW, I AM going to teach you the four steps on how to make a right decision. First of all, you have got to **get over it.** Too often you don't make right decisions because you haven't gotten over the wrong ones you have made. Then you haven't gotten beyond the wall that was there. It's time to **get beyond it.** Stop looking back to the wall instead of to Jesus, who is the answer.

How do we make a right decision? We want you to get it right for life, and it's a simple process, but you have got to do it. When we make right choices, God says in Proverbs 2:20:

> *"Stay on the right path.*
> *Don't look to the right.*
> *Don't look to the left.*
> *Stay on the right path."*

I am going to give you the four steps for making right choices. These are critical steps. You have got to understand these steps because if you don't go through these steps you are going to make wrong choices. Many of you know what's right, but you are making wrong choices because you don't process it correctly. I helped develop this process in the midst of writing a curriculum called, *Truth Matters.*

Step 1: **Consider the choice.**

> *"The simple believes every word, but the prudent considers well his steps. A wise man fears and departs from evil, but a fool rages and is self-confident. A quick-tempered man acts foolishly, and a man of wicked intentions is hated."* (Proverbs 14:15-17)

Now the key word in this text is *consider.* "*Consider* the choice." It's being proactive instead of reactive. When something happens and you react to it, you will be foolish because you will react based on feelings, experience or based on your circumstances. And when you react, you are usually wrong.

Think about it. Somebody says something to you, and you just react to him or her. Usually what comes out is the flesh. And the reason the flesh comes out is because you are not proactive. You have not considered the choice before it happens. Being proactive is considering the choices ahead of you before you ever get there. Then if you get to a choice that you have not considered or instead of reacting to it, you step back, and you look at the whole picture.

Stop – Look - Listen. You learned that as a child. You need to do it as an adult.

Stop – Look - Listen. Don't make the decision yet. Look at the entire scope of the situation - particularly at the long-term consequences.

> "If I say this or do this, how will this affect my life in five years?"

Every day is filled with choices. You must decide to follow God before the temptations arise. We must agree with Joshua at this point:

> "…Serve the LORD! And if it seems evil to you to serve the LORD, choose for yourselves this day whom you will serve,

…But as for me and my house, we will serve the LORD"
(Joshua 24:14-15).

I worked with a pastor who had a one-night stand a couple of years ago. He called me up and said, "Larry, my marriage is in a mess."

I said, "Really? What happened?"

He said, "I had a one-night stand. I was at the convenience store, and there was a hooker there. She propositioned me, and for a moment, I forgot who I was.

I thought, "My God, you never knew who you were. You didn't forget. You never became the person God wanted you to be."

He said, "And then I knew I was wrong. I went home and I repented to my wife."

Now, that was a good thing. You deal with sin quickly. One of A.W. Tozer's five spiritual vows is that you deal with sin quickly. His wife was able to handle it better than he was. His church fired him.

Then he came to me and said, "What did I do wrong? I repented. I went to the church."

I said, "What you did wrong was that you didn't consider the choice before you even when into the convenience store."

If I go into the convenience store, and there is a hooker there, I am going to try to get her saved, but I am not going to try to get her in bed. I have considered the choice. Are you following what I am saying here? I know how I am going to react.

Men, read this carefully. The number one problem in America is pornography – internet pornography with men. And you can't stop the spams. It is almost impossible to have a perfect blocker for these spam artists. So when the internet message comes through, the question isn't whether you are going to go to the link or not. It is whether you are going to pause and think about it before you delete it.

Consider the choice. Step back and look at all the options. Take the long look. Consider the choice. Don't react quickly. Stop, look and listen.

Step 2: Compare to God.

Here's the second step. Every day is going to be filled with choices. Let's go on. Choose this day - What are you going to do? Don't play the comparison game. The second step is to compare your options or your choices to God. Don't play this comparison game.

"What will others think? What will others do? Will others be upset with me?"

Others don't make any difference. You have to ask yourself, "Who am I trying to please?" And if you want to have a clue, the album or the CD that the worship team has done says it all. You have just One in your audience on this one, folks. His name is God.

"I wonder what my wife would think."

Irrelevant.

"I wonder what my husband or my parents would think."

It's of no consequence what they think. You are to live your life pleasing God and not men. So you compare to God.

Now watch this. I didn't say compare to Scripture. And the reason I didn't say to compare it to the Word is because when you start comparing it to the Word what happens is you become a legalist. I want to tell you something. Anybody who wants to play the con game can find any scripture in here to justify any action.

"Well, I murdered him because I went to the Bible. The Bible says that Cain killed Abel. It must be okay. It's in the Bible."

Remember these truths:

- Scripture can become rules and we become defense lawyers pleading our case.
- God is always right—absolute truths are biblical principles from the **whole counsel of God**. (Acts 20:27)
- We must stand on absolute truth not relativism.
- Absolute truth is what's true for all people, all times and in all situations.

And the LORD spoke to Moses, saying, "Speak to all the congregation of the children of Israel, and say to them: **'You shall be holy, for I the LORD your God am holy'**" (Leviticus 19:1-3).

So, you are holy because He is holy.

The reason that you are pure isn't because you don't want to affect others or yourself with your sin. It's bigger than that. You are pure because God is pure. You are holy because God is holy. You are the temple of the Holy Spirit; do you not know it? The Spirit of God indwells you, and that means His character is in you.

I will never forget this. I asked my son Peter a question. We were working on a curriculum based on the book, *Right From Wrong,* and Peter walked through the room. I said, "Peter, I know you have made a decision to be pure before marriage - to have abstinence as your guideline. Why?"

He said, "Dad, are you writing a book?"

I said, "Yeah."

He said, "Am I going to be in the book?"

I said, "Yeah."

He said, "So, I've got to answer this right?"

I say, "Of course."

"Because the Bible says, 'flee immorality.'"

"Great, Peter," I replied. "Why else?"

"Because I want to save my purity for my wife."

"Wonderful," I answered. "Why else?"

"Because if you found out I wasn't pure, you'd kill me!" he shouted and walked out of the room.

I explained later to Peter that the reason he stayed pure was that God was pure and holy. The living God lived in him. Therefore, his desire to be holy and pure came from God Himself.

Step 3: Choose the right.

When you know what is right and don't do it, it's sin (James 4:17). When we know what the right is, we must NOT procrastinate or make excuses. We must ACT! Listen to what God says:

> "I call heaven and earth as witnesses today against you, that I have set before you life and death, blessing and cursing; **therefore choose life,** that both you and your descendants may live; that you may love the LORD your God, that you may obey His voice, and that you may cling to Him, for He is your life and the length of your days" (Deuteronomy 30:19-20).

So what keeps us from choosing what's right?

- **Ignorance** (We perish for lack of knowledge.)
- **Rebellion** (I do what I want.)
- **Fear** (I fear risk & change so I choose comfort, relief and consequences.
- **The Past** (I can't let go of the past in order to grasp God's future & hope.)
- **Procrastination** (I'll wait just a bit longer and see what may happen.")

All these things can keep you from choosing what is right. I want to just give you a quick list.

Ignorance. You don't know what's right. People perish because of a lack of knowledge. I want to tell you something. When you have a decision to make, Bishop is not going to be there whispering in your ear. You are going to have to know the Bible for yourself. You are going to have to know God for yourself. You are going to have to get it right. It's between you and God right now.

Rebellion. Some of you are just plain out rebellious. The reason you make wrong decisions is because you are rebelling against God. He is asking for your obedience in this matter.

Fear. Some of you can't do what's right because you are fearful. You fear risk and change, and so you choose comfort and relief, and then you suffer the consequences. Most of you don't like repentance because it hurts. You have got to change. So you ask for relief, and you never change. You want God to be a Tylenol instead of a surgeon.

The Past and Procrastination. Some of you are still in the past and a few of you love to procrastinate. You can do the right thing at the wrong time and have a huge mess on your hands - a huge problem on your plate. Right?

The Holy Spirit gives you the power to overcome hindrances to doing what's right. Let Him empower you to choose the right!

Step 4: Count the cost!

> "For which of you, intending to build a tower, does not sit down first and **count the cost**, whether he has enough to finish it" (Luke 14:28).

After we choose the right, we must count the cost. No man builds a tower who doesn't first sit down and count the cost whether he has enough to finish it or not. Every right decision will cost you something.

So, when I have a decision to make, I am going to consider the choice. I am going to step back. I am going to look at it. I am going to take the long look. Then I am going to compare my options to God and choose what reflects His character, His holiness, His grace, His truth, and His purity. Then I am going to move on, and I am going to actually do it. Some of you are missing the season of your blessing because you are procrastinating, and you are not doing the right thing now.

And finally, I am going to count the cost. I am willing to pay the price. I don't care what it costs me. I don't care what the sacrifice is. I may lose everything, but I will lose it all to gain Him.

> *"For whosoever will save his life shall lose it; but whosoever shall lose his life for my sake and the gospel's, the same shall save it. For what shall it profit a man, if he shall gain the whole world, and lose his own soul? Or what shall a man give in exchange for his soul?"* (Mark 8:35-37 KJV)

It's time, right now, for you to get over it…
So that you can get beyond it…
In order to get it right for the rest of your life by making right decisions

CHOOSE THE RIGHT, NOW!

I HAVE GOOD news for you. You can get over it in order to get beyond it so that you can get it right for the rest of your life.

God is giving you, by the Holy Spirit, the power to consider your choices, to compare them to God and to choose what's right. Stop procrastinating. Count the cost and be willing to pay the price no matter what it is. Because, when you are choosing what's right today, it shapes your future. Not only does it shape your future, it also shapes your family's future. It shapes your children's future. It shapes your grandchildren's future.

There was a brief moment in our marriage where we considered the choice of divorce or not. And if we had taken the wrong choice, Asher, Judah, Stone, Jade and Jasmine would not be in our lives today—our grandchildren. Because our children's lives would have been turned upside down. We would have never moved to where we were supposed to move. We would have never done what we were supposed to have done. Our children would have never been in the right place.

You see, our decision wasn't just about us. It was about them. In fact, it's never about us. It's always about our spiritual and our natural children. It's about our seed and our seed's seed. It's about leaving a good inheritance for our seed's seed.

God wants you to do that, and here is the way you start: *you make right choices.*

Right now, you may be facing a choice and you desperately need God. Without the right choice, your future is in jeopardy. I don't know what the choice is. But I know Who the answer is, and He is by your side right now. Jesus is with you. The Holy Spirit, the Teacher of all Truth, is guiding you. He wants to give you the power to make right choices.

If you are facing a choice and you desperately need God's input, I want you to pray, "God, I have to make a choice right now. I need You, God. I desperately need God. God, I want to compare this choice to You. God I want to choose what's right. In Jesus Name. Amen."

So, you can consider the choice and choose the right. Choose the right. I am praying for you,

> *Heavenly Father, in Jesus' Name, I pray for the Spirit of Truth, the Holy Spirit, to fill you and to give you the boldness to consider the choice, to compare it to God, to choose what's right, to count the cost, to be willing to pay whatever the price is because, Father, the future rests on this choice. And it's going to be right because, Lord God, You are in it. In Jesus' Name, Amen.*[13]

Endnotes

1   Jeremiah 29:11 paraphrased

2   Duckworth, Angela Ph.D. Grit: The Passion of Power and Perseverance New York: Simon and Schuster 2016, 2019 p. 95

3   liveboldandbloom.com/01/self-improvement/grit-quotes

4   Grit: The Power of Passion and Perseverance New York: Scribner Books 2016, p.273.

5   1 Thessalonians 5;16-18 NIV

6   Ephesians 6:10-13

7   Katy Milkman. How to Change: The Science of Getting from Where You Are to Where You Want to Be New York: Penguin Random House 2021 p.192.

8   https://www.brainyquote.com/topics/falling-quotes

9   Grit: The Power of Passion and Perseverance, p. 137.

10 https://www.womenshealthmag.com/relationships/a33297780/what-are-the-five-love-languages/?utm_source=google&utm_medium=cpc&utm_campaign=arb_ga_whm_md_pmx_us_urlx&gclid=CjwKCAjwsfuYBhAZEiwA5a6CDP_I6Evbey-WB_iVgqm-bVhY1tUYx__1CHMqWWvJKvxJb2oJvUWiCjBoCTX-gQAvD_BwE

11 1 Thessalonians 5:16-18

12 @CorporateCouch

13 Adapted from an unpublished message by Dr. Larry Keefauver and used with permission. This teaching really resonates with my life story, and I know it will benefit you, the reader.

www.ingramcontent.com/pod-product-compliance
Lightning Source LLC
LaVergne TN
LVHW071355250125
802036LV00008B/27